Smith Family Bookstore

TEXT JUL 2 2 2007

New.

AUG 1 6 2004

New

Gender Diversity

Crosscultural Variations

Serena Nanda

John Jay College of Criminal Justice

WAVELAND
PRESS, INC.

Long Grove, Illinois

For information about this book, write or call:
Waveland Press, Inc.
4180 IL Route 83, Suite 101
Long Grove, IL 60047-9580
(847) 634-0081
info@waveland.com
www.waveland.com

Cover Photograph: Kathoey, or transgendered males, are featured performers in transvestite revues. (Photograph by Ravinder Nanda.)

Copyright © 2000 by Serena Nanda

ISBN 1-57766-074-9

All rights reserved. No part of this book may be reproduced, stored in a retrieval system, or transmitted in any form or by any means without permission in writing from the publisher.

Printed in the United States of America

10   9   8   7   6   5   4

Contents

Contents

Preface

This book, based on ethnographic data of gender diversity in seven cultures, is an introduction to the subject of gender diversity. It is aimed at students in gender studies, human sexuality, cultural anthropology, and gay and lesbian studies. The ethnographic material is set in the context of the main theoretical issues which inform the contemporary study of gender diversity. These issues are outlined in the Introduction. In addition to a glossary and references, an annotated filmography is included.

This book is made possible because of the outstanding ethnographies and histories that have been published on alternative gender roles in the last twenty years. These authors are identified in the text and have my unstinting admiration. In addition, I am profoundly grateful to my friends and colleagues who have encouraged my own work in gender diversity and been so generous in sharing their ideas with me. Only space limitations prevent more personal acknowledgment of their contributions: Santos Berenato, Niko Besnier, Jasper Burns, Joan Gregg, Kelley Hayes, Gilbert Herdt, Martin Manalansan IV, Linda Meyers, Jill Norgren, Russell Oberlin, Gayatri Reddy, John Reid, Will Roscoe, Tobias Schneebaum, Michael Sweet, Randolph Trumbach and Unni Wikan. I also wish to thank Caroline Brettell, Richley Crapo and Alice Kehoe for their thoughtful and helpful reviews of the manuscript. I am grateful to the PSC-CUNY Research Foundation for partial funding of my fieldwork on the hijras; the Park Ridge Center for the Study of Health, Faith, and Ethics in Chicago for funding my participation in their symposium on Religion and Sexuality; and members of the staff and administration of John Jay College of Criminal Justice, particularly Linda John, of the Department of Anthropology, for the essential support services that moved this book toward publication. Jeni Ogilvie, my editor at Waveland, was immeasurably helpful and I am very appreciative of her contribution. She was a pleasure to work with. Finally, I want to thank Tom Curtin of Waveland Press, a long-time friend and colleague. Through his commitment to presenting anthropological research to undergraduate students in an interesting and accessible format, Tom and Waveland Press have made an invaluable contribution to the discipline of cultural anthropology.

Introduction

In contemporary Euro-American cultures sex and gender ideologies are based on binary opposites—male and female, man and woman, homosexual and heterosexual, indeed the binary opposition of sex and gender itself. Although many anthropologists argue that binary thinking is part of human nature, and that the male/female binary is among the most basic thought patterns of human culture, sex and gender binaries are not universal and in fact have not always dominated European culture. *Gender diversity* (which I use interchangeably with gender variation) refers to the fact that cultures construct their sex and gender systems differently and that these systems do not always neatly divide into male and female, man and woman.

Anthropological studies of gender diversity are significant in their own right and are also important in gender studies more generally. Anthropology's crosscultural approach enables us to think about behavior, attitudes, and perceptions of sex, gender, and sexuality that are not part of our own experience. The anthropological perspective cautions us against making any easy generalizations about "human nature." Because sex, gender, and sexuality are at the very core of individual identity in modern Western culture, it is difficult to dislodge our ideas, and more so, our feelings, about them. The examples of gender diversity in this book challenge intellectual understandings about what is natural, normal, and morally right and also challenge us at deeper emotional and personal levels.

A crosscultural perspective makes it clear that there are many different (though probably not unlimited) ways that societies can organize their thinking about sex, gender, and sexuality. All the cultures described here provide spaces for sex and gender roles beyond the binary opposites of male and female, man and woman. Each culture is different from the others and I have tried (not completely successfully) to avoid a division between "the West" and "the rest."

1

The cultures represented here do not encompass the total range of sex and gender diversity. Some important examples, such as the male transgendered *xanith* of Oman (Wikan 1977) and woman-woman marriage and female husbands in Africa (e.g., Amadiume 1987; Oboler 1980; Roscoe and Murray 1998), are regretfully omitted due to space limitations. I chose my examples because they are ethnographically well documented and because they represent diverse geographical areas and cultural patterns of sex and gender diversity.

SOME BASIC DEFINITIONS

In order to understand gender diversity, a grasp of some basic issues and definitions, particularly sex, gender, and sexuality, are necessary. **Sex** refers to the biologically differentiated status of male or female. It includes anatomic sex, particularly the genitals, and also secondary and invisible characteristics such as genes and hormones. **Gender** refers to the social, cultural, and psychological constructions that are imposed upon the biological differences of sex.

The concept of gender as developed by social scientists has been useful in challenging the view that biological sex determines the roles and attributes of men and women in society. But this concept also resulted in a dichotomy: biological sex (the opposition of male and female) was viewed as "natural" and universal, and gender (the opposition of man and woman) was viewed as culturally learned and variable. This opposition between sex and gender made an important contribution in undermining biological determinism, especially in the study of women's roles, but is now being challenged on the basis that biological sex is also an idea mediated only through culture (see especially Butler 1990:6).

The ethnographic record makes it clear that there is no simple, universal, inevitable, or "correct" correspondence between sex and gender and that the Euro-American privileging of biological sex (anatomy) is not universal. Many cultures do not make the distinction between the natural and the cultural or between sex and gender; for many cultures, anatomical sex is not the dominant factor in constructing gender roles and gender identity. In addition, opposing the terms sex and gender overlooks the integration of biology and culture in human life, experience, and behavior. Thus, I generally use the term sex/gender (as in sex/gender systems, sex/gender roles, or sex/gender ideologies) unless the opposition of sex and gender is an explicit and significant element in the cultural pattern under discussion.

Sexuality, another critical concept in the study of gender diversity, can refer to erotic desires, sexual practices, or sexual orientation. Western understandings of sexuality have been inappropriately imposed on other cultures. This is particularly true regarding **homosexuality**. In contemporary Euro-American culture individuals are socially identified as homosexuals or heterosexuals as if one's **sexual orientation** encapsulated one's total personality and identity. In contrast to this cultural pattern, in many cultures, "the homosexual" and "the **heterosexual**" as social identities do not exist. In addition, many cultures do not identify both partners in same-sex sexual relations as homosexual, but only the partner whose sexual role is opposite to his or her anatomy. Thus, in male same-sex sexual relationships only the partner who takes the receptor role in anal sex is culturally marked, and the "male" or active partner is not considered different from other men. In some of these cultures, in a pattern called **gendered homosexuality**, the male partner taking the "feminine" role in sex adopts other feminine characteristics and may be reclassified as to sex/gender status (Murray 1995:11). It is important to keep in mind that this text is *not* about homosexuality in its contemporary Euro-American sense as an identity shared by all persons whose preference is for sexual partners of the same sex. Rather, this text is about gender diversity, whose relation to sexuality varies across cultures. The frequent Euro-American misidentification of gender diversity with homosexuality has led to misunderstandings of other sex/gender systems and to misplaced judgments of other cultures as immoral or uncivilized.

Gender diversity occupies different places in different cultures. While all of the variant sex/gender roles described in this text are linguistically differentiated from the roles of male and female, man and woman, some of these variant roles are relatively more coherent and well defined—that is, more *institutionalized*—and well integrated into the cultural pattern than others. Cultures also vary in the extent to which gender diversity has sacred or spiritual associations. In India, for example, persons crossing or bridging sex/gender boundaries are considered inherently powerful or auspicious, while in Polynesia or the United States, alternative sex/gender roles are basically secular.

Because cultures attach different meanings to sex/gender diversity, these roles must always be analyzed in connection with other cultural patterns, particularly the dominant sex/gender ideology. Even in multigendered cultures, gender diversity always exists against a background of what it means to be male or female, man or woman in a particular society. In addition, while broader cultural patterns illuminate the meanings of gender diversity, understandings of gender diversity illuminate other aspects of a sex/gender system.

SOCIAL ATTITUDES TOWARD
SEX/GENDER DIVERSITY

Much Western writing has romanticized and idealized non-Western cultures' seemingly positive valuation of sex/gender diversity, the latitude they allow for the expression of gender variation or the integration of alternatively gendered individuals into society. Relatively speaking, gender variance has not been as severely sanctioned in some other cultures as it has been in many Western societies. Idealization distorts the ethnographic record, however, when it assumes, inaccurately, that sex/gender variation in non-Western or nonindustrialized societies is always highly valued and that gender nonconformists are not marginalized, stigmatized, or discriminated against.

Idealization obscures the reality that in most societies, certainly most contemporary societies, attitudes toward gender diversity are ambivalent and complicated. Such attitudes include awe, fear, respect, ridicule, disgust, dismay, pity, bemusement, and often a contradictory combination of these emotions. Even in societies like India and Brazil, or among North American Indians, where gender diversity is associated with ritual powers, attitudes toward gender variants in ordinary social interaction is ambivalent and even sometimes hostile.

Furthermore, a positive or tolerant attitude toward gender diversity in the past does not necessarily translate into acceptance of gender diversity in the present. Historically, for example, American Indian multigender systems often valued gender diversity, but contemporary gay and lesbian individuals may face stigma and discrimination on Indian reservations.

Hostile social attitudes toward gender diversity, specialized occupations associated with gender variants, and other factors may lead to the spatial segregation of gender variants and/or the development of subcultures and social communities. In Indian, Brazilian, Filipino, European and American cities, for example, gender variant individuals often live and work in specific locations, facilitating the development of subcultures. The degree to which gender diversity is associated with spatially bounded social groups or specialized subcultures may well be a function of population size, as these formations are largely absent in the smaller and less socially specialized societies such as historic American Indian, precolonial Filipino, Polynesian, or Balkan cultures.

Attitudes toward gender diversity vary within cultures as well as between them. Age, region, social class, educational level, ethnicity, religion, urban or rural residence, exposure to Western cultures, and gender itself are all factors influencing attitudes toward gender diversity. In addition, social attitudes toward gender diversity are always somewhat different than attitudes gender variant individuals have about themselves, especially when social attitudes are negative.

While cultural images of gender diversity influence how individuals see themselves, there are also important individual differences in *sex/gender identity* (how one experiences oneself as a sexed and gendered person). This individual variation is based on differences in personality, life circumstances, social class, and other factors and helps explain variation in recruitment to gender variant roles. Individuals vary in how they play alternatively gendered roles and how they challenge or manipulate cultural norms as they try to adapt to their societies.

Ethnographic (and perhaps more so, psychological) descriptions of sex/gender identity tend to give a more static picture of sex/gender identity than is actually the case. Although the term identity implies a certain consistency or continuity in subjective experience, identities are dynamic; they change with the situation or frame of reference and change over time. Even the most institutionalized sex/gender identities are always more varied than a focus on cultural norms alone would imply.

SEXUALITY AND GENDER DIVERSITY

Significant cultural variation occurs in what is considered appropriate sexuality—desire, orientation, practices—for different genders and in the presumed relationship between sex/gender diversity, sexuality, and gender identity. Sexual orientation, for example, is an important part of social identity (individuals are categorized as homosexuals or heterosexuals) in contemporary Euro-American cultures, but is no longer associated with gender diversity as it was in the eighteenth, nineteenth, and early-twentieth centuries. In contemporary Euro-American cultures, the relationship between sexuality and *transsexuals* and between sexuality and *transgenderists* varies widely among individuals. (The "sex" in transsexualism refers to anatomy, not sexuality.) In Brazil sexuality is central to gender variance, but it is sexual practice—position in sexual intercourse—and not sexual orientation alone that determines one's place in the sex/gender system. This is also true to some extent in Thailand and the Philippines. In contrast, in Polynesia and among American Indians, sexuality is less important than occupation in defining sex/gender diversity, while in India, in the European Middle Ages, and in the Balkans, it is the renunciation of sexuality that defines both male and female gender variant roles. One of the more frequent forms of gender diversity crossculturally involves transgendered males, that is, men who identify with and/or act like women, including in their sexuality. But even this common form of gender diversity is differently understood in different cultures.

The frequent association of male gender diversity with prostitution and sexual "deviance," especially as part of an international sex work industry, complicates the picture of the nature of male transgendered sexuality. Researchers have generally underestimated and underreported the role of sexual desire in commercial sex, and Western culture focuses on the commercial aspects of prostitution as if it were a simple "selling of the body." Although we can never overlook the association of prostitution with poverty, the exchange of sex for money is culturally variable, and needs also to be viewed as part of a complex system of culturally motivated transactions in which symbolic and emotional exchanges are also relevant.

Nevertheless, the association between prostitution and transgendered males compounds social hostility toward gender variants (see Magerl 2000), as does the association between sex/gender diversity and AIDS. At the same time, the association with Westeners that sex work often entails may bring some prestige. The income from prostitution is also sometimes translated into symbols of high social status or used to gain social acceptance within the families of gender variants, who may lean on them for economic support.

GLOBALIZATION AND GENDER DIVERSITY

Culture contact is an important source of change in sex/gender ideologies and identities. Throughout the contemporary world and, since the first European encounters with non-European cultures, ideologies of sex/gender diversity have been influenced, changed, and, as in the pre-contact Philippines and American Indian societies, practically destroyed. This diffusion of Euro-American culture continues today through tourism (including international sex tourism), the global media, and the spread of academic and scientific discourses. In all the cultures described in this book, Euro-American sex/gender identities, such as "gay" and "lesbian," have become incorporated into traditional sex/gender ideologies, though often in ways that change their original meanings. The widespread incorporation of Western ideas means that in most societies today several sex/gender systems—indigenous and foreign—operate simultaneously, with gender variant individuals moving between and among them as they try to construct their lives in meaningful and positive ways.

Cultural influences spread in many directions, however. The sex/gender ideologies of other cultures also influence those of the West, significantly through the medium of anthropological representation. The crosscultural data of anthropology, demonstrating that sex/gender identities and roles are understood differently in different cultures, have found their way back into Euro-American culture as one of the important sources of the transgender movement, the gay rights movement, and the increasing willingness of the larger society to understand, and perhaps even appreciate, sex/gender diversity.

FEMALE GENDER DIVERSITY

Because of the more complete ethnographic and historical record, this text mainly focuses on patterns of gender diversity in which biological males in some way act like or are culturally identified as "like women." In part this record reflects the cultural emphasis of most societies. For reasons that are not completely clear but involve (among others) socialization (child rearing), patriarchy, and biology, male gender variance occurs more frequently and is more frequently culturally emphasized than female gender variance. The anthropological literature, for example, suggests that "achieving manhood" is a more difficult process and is more surrounded by ritual than "achieving womanhood" (see Chodorow 1974; Gilmore 1990; Herdt 1981). In patriarchal societies, the social status gained by transgendered women appears less threatening to society than the social status lost by transgendered men and helps account for the cultural focus on male gender nonconformity (Bullough and Bullough 1993:46).

On the other hand, some of the ethnographic and historical emphasis on male gender variance results from gender bias, as male researchers (or observers) may be denied access to females and/or had less interest in recording their behavior. In early modern Europe, for example, male sodomy was a crime that left a rich archive of court records; this is not available for women, whose same-sex sexual relations were not as severely legally sanctioned. In addition, in many cultures "manly" behavior by females can be incorporated within the culturally defined roles of women in a way that is not true for men; in some cultures, for example Polynesia, elderly women are treated as similar to men.

Female same-sex sexual desire and practices are culturally less visible than those of men. Though this subject is now getting greater attention (see Blackwood and Wieringa 1999; Penrose 2001), it is not associated with gender diversity to the extent that is true of males. Clearly, however, female gender diversity has its own cultural dynamic and is not simply a derivative, a parallel, or the reverse, of male gender diversity.

For the cultures described here, female gender variant roles were found most frequently in North American Indian societies, though not as frequently as for males; a survey of those roles and some examples are included in the chapter. In India, a female gender variant role is described, though such roles are much less visible and less widespread

than male roles. In Polynesia, women can be included in the gender variant category, although this is almost completely unrecorded in the historical and anthropological literature. In Thailand gender diversity was
historically associated with females as well as males, but is now associated mainly with males. In Euro-American cultures transsexualism,
once culturally represented only through males, now includes an
increasing number of females, as does the newest form of gender diversity, transgenderism. In the Euro-American chapter, I describe two
female gender variant roles, both of which center on virginity, one from
the European Middle Ages and the other from nineteenth- and early-
twentieth-century culture in the Balkans.

BOOK OUTLINE

    Chapter 1, "Multiple Genders among North American Indians,"
surveys gender variance in native North America as it was historically
documented during the period 1860–1930. Gender diversity existed
throughout the Americas; since most classic anthropological analysis
applies to North America, this region forms the ethnographic core of this
chapter. For reasons that are not entirely clear, North American Indian
societies appear to have supported the widest range of genuine multigender systems. The extent to which such sex/gender diversity continues
today is a source of debate.

    Chapter 2 describes the male gender variant role of the *hijras* and
a female gender variant role, the *sādhin*. Both roles are grounded in the
Hindu religious tradition of asceticism. Unlike American Indian multigender systems, where gender diversity was also religiously grounded,
however, India's gender diversity is built on a sex/gender system in
which male and female, man and woman, are sharply differentiated and
hierarchically related.

    Brazil, described in chapter 3, is an extension of the "Mediterra-
nean" pattern of gendered homosexuality, in which gender is experienced
in the sexual distinction between those who penetrate and those who are
penetrated. This distinction primarily operates in secular contexts but
also has ritual associations within Afro-Brazilian religions.

    Chapter 4 describes "liminal" sex/gender roles in Polynesia. In con-
trast to the religious and institutionalized nature of sex/gender diversity
in North American Indian cultures, Hindu India, and Brazil, in Polynesia sex/gender diversity is less institutionalized and to a large extent
defined by performances staged for entertainment purposes.

    Secular performance is also central to sex/gender diversity in con-
temporary Thailand and the Philippines, described in chapter 5. While
not unique in Asia, Thailand and the Philippines share an important

similarity: in both cultures gender diversity is currently mainly constructed as male transgendered homosexuality. Both cultures have been significantly influenced by contact with Western cultural concepts and are today characterized by multiple sex/gender ideologies that sometimes overlap or contradict each other.

In chapter 6, I explore Euro-American gender diversity as it has changed historically—and in cycles—in the perceived relationship between sex/gender diversity and sexuality. Before the eighteenth and nineteenth centuries same-sex sexual practices and orientation were associated with multiple genders, and the binary oppositions of male and female, man and woman, heterosexual and homosexual did not hold the dominant position they do today. Within this context of historical change, I examine two earlier forms of female sex/gender diversity, the transvestite saint and the "sworn virgin," as well as the more contemporary transition from transsexualism to transgenderism.

The final chapter, "Variations on a Theme," summarizes some of the more important concepts discussed in the ethnographic chapters.

ANTHROPOLOGY AND CULTURAL DIFFERENCE

Describing crosscultural variations of sex/gender diversity highlights the different meanings attached to this diversity in different cultures. The crosscultural perspective raises our consciousness about the *cultural construction* of sex, gender, and sexualities and their relationship to each other in all cultures. This emphasis on difference illuminates how sex/gender ideologies are experienced as identities that are practically unimaginable to people in different cultures. The focus on cultural difference also emphasizes that there is no one correct or superior way to organize sex/gender categories or to treat sex/gender nonconformity.

If anthropology is about difference, however, it is also about bridging difference. In the classical anthropological tradition of looking at "other cultures" from the inside, and one's own culture from the outside, we are enabled to cross the barriers of cultural difference to a recognition of a greater shared humanity. This is the heart of cultural anthropology as a humanistic as well as a scientific discipline.

Chapter One

Multiple Genders among North American Indians

The early encounters between Europeans and Indian societies in the New World, in the fifteenth through the seventeenth centuries, brought together cultures with very different sex/gender systems. The Spanish explorers, coming from a society where sodomy was a heinous crime, were filled with contempt and outrage when they recorded the presence of men in American Indian societies who performed the work of women, dressed like women, and had sexual relations with men (Lang 1996; Roscoe in 1995).

Europeans labelled these men "berdache," a term originally derived from an Arabic word meaning male prostitute. As such, this term is inappropriate and insulting, and I use it here only to indicate the history of European (mis)understanding of American Indian sex/gender diversity. The term berdache focused attention on the sexuality associated with mixed gender roles, which the Europeans identified, incorrectly, with the "unnatural" and sinful practice of sodomy in their own societies. In their ethnocentrism, the early European explorers and colonists were unable to see beyond their own sex/gender systems and thus did not understand the multiple sex/gender systems they encountered in the Americas. They also largely overlooked the specialized and spiritual functions of many of these alternative sex/gender roles and the positive value attached to them in many American Indian societies.

By the late-nineteenth and early-twentieth centuries, some anthropologists included accounts of North American Indian sex/gender diversity in their ethnographies. They attempted to explain the berdache from various functional perspectives, that is, in terms of the contributions these sex/gender roles made to social structure or culture. These accounts, though less contemptuous than earlier ones, nevertheless

largely retained the emphasis on berdache sexuality. The berdache was
defined as a form of "institutionalized homosexuality," which served as a
social niche for individuals whose personality and sexual orientation did
not match the definition of masculinity in their societies, or as a "way
out" of the masculine or warrior role for "cowardly" or "failed" men (see
Callender and Kochems 1983).

Anthropological accounts increasingly paid more attention, however, to the association of the berdache with shamanism and spiritual
powers and also noted that mixed gender roles were often central and
highly valued in American Indian cultures, rather than marginal and
deviant. These accounts were, nevertheless, also ethnocentric in misi-
dentifying indigenous gender diversity with European concepts of homosexuality, transvestism, or hermaphroditism, which continued to distort
their indigenous meanings.

In American Indian societies, the European homosexual/heterosex-
ual dichotomy was not culturally relevant and the European labeling of the
berdache as homosexuals resulted from their own cultural emphasis on
sexuality as a central, even defining, aspect of gender and on sodomy as an
abnormal practice and/or a sin. While berdache in many American Indian
societies did engage in sexual relations and even married persons of the
same sex, this was not central to their alternative gender role. Another
overemphasis resulting from European ethnocentrism was the identification of berdache as *transvestites*. Although berdache often cross-dressed,
transvestism was not consistent within or across societies. European
descriptions of berdache as *hermaphrodites* were also inaccurate.

Considering the variation in alternative sex/gender roles in native
North America, a working definition may be useful: the berdache in the
anthropological literature refers to people who partly or completely take
on aspects of the culturally defined role of the other sex and who are classified neither as women nor men, but as genders of their own (see Callender and Kochems 1983:443). It is important to note here that berdache thus refers to variant gender roles, rather than a complete crossing over to an opposite gender role.

In the past twenty-five years there have been important shifts in
perspectives on sex/gender diversity among American Indians and
anthropologists, both Indian and non-Indian (Jacobs, Thomas, and Lang
1997:Introduction). Most current research rejects institutionalized
homosexuality as an adequate explanation of American Indian gender
diversity, emphasizing the importance of occupation rather than sexuality as its central feature. Contemporary ethnography views multiple sex/
gender roles as a normative part of American Indian sex/gender systems,
rather than as a marginal or deviant part (Albers 1989:134; Jacobs et al.
1997; Lang 1998). A new emphasis on the variety of alternative sex/gen-
der roles in North America undercuts the earlier treatment of the ber-

dache as a unitary phenomenon across North (and South) America (Callender and Kochems 1983; Jacobs et al. 1997; Lang 1998; Roscoe 1998). Current research also emphasizes the integrated and often highly valued position of gender variant persons and the association of sex/gender diversity with spiritual power (Roscoe 1996; Williams 1992).

A change in terminology has also taken place. Berdache generally has been rejected, but there is no unanimous agreement on what should replace it. One widely accepted suggestion is the term *two-spirit* (Jacobs et al. 1997; Lang 1998), a term coined in 1990 by urban American Indian gays and lesbians. Two-spirit has the advantage of conveying the spiritual nature of gender variance as viewed by gay, lesbian, and transgendered American Indians and also the spirituality associated with traditional American Indian gender variance, but the cultural continuity suggested by two-spirit is in fact a subject of debate. Another problem is that two-spirit emphasizes the Euro-American gender construction of only two genders. Thus, I use the more culturally neutral term, variant genders (or gender variants) and specific indigenous terms wherever possible.

DISTRIBUTION AND CHARACTERISTICS
OF VARIANT SEX/GENDER ROLES

Multiple sex/gender systems were found in many, though not all, American Indian societies. Male gender variant roles (variant gender roles assumed by biological males) are documented for 110 to 150 societies. These roles occurred most frequently in the region extending from California to the Mississippi Valley and upper-Great Lakes, the Plains and the Prairies, the Southwest, and to a lesser extent along the Northwest Coast tribes. With few exceptions, gender variance is not historically documented for eastern North America, though it may have existed prior to European invasion and disappeared before it could be recorded historically (Callender and Kochems 1983; Fulton and Anderson 1992).

There were many variations in North American Indian gender diversity. American Indian cultures included three or four genders: men, women, male variants, and female variants (biological females who by engaging in male activities were reclassified as to gender). Gender variant roles differed in the criteria by which they were defined; the degree of their integration into the society; the norms governing their behavior; the way the role was acknowledged publicly or sanctioned; how others were expected to behave toward gender variant persons; the degree to which a gender changer was expected to adopt the role of the opposite sex or was limited in doing so; the power, sacred or secular, that was attributed to them; and the path to recruitment.

Berdache, by Joe
Lawrence Lembo, 1987.
(Tempera on paper,
18x24.)

In spite of this variety, however, there were also some common or widespread features: transvestism, cross-gender occupation, same sex (but different gender) sexuality, some culturally normative and acknowledged process for recruitment to the role, special language and ritual roles, and associations with spiritual power.

TRANSVESTISM

The degree to which male and female gender variants were permitted to wear the clothing of the other sex varied. Transvestism was often associated with gender variance but was not equally important in all societies. Male gender variants frequently adopted women's dress and hairstyles partially or completely, and female gender variants partially adopted the clothing of men; sometimes, however, transvestism was prohibited. The choice of clothing was sometimes an individual matter and gender variants might mix their clothing and their accoutrements. For example, a female gender variant might wear a woman's dress but carry (male) weapons. Dress was also sometimes situationally determined: a male gender variant would have to wear men's clothing while engaging in warfare but might wear women's clothes at other times. Similarly, female gender variants might wear women's clothing when gathering (women's work), but male clothing when hunting (men's work) (Callender and Kochems 1983:447). Among the Navajo, a male gender variant, **nádleeh**, would adopt almost all aspects of a woman's dress, work, language and behavior; the Mohave male gender variant, called **alyha**, was at the extreme end of the cross-gender continuum in imitating female physiology as well as transvestism (the transvestite ceremony is discussed later in this chapter). Repression of visible forms of gender diversity, and ultimately the almost total decline of transvestism, were a direct result of American prohibitions against it.

OCCUPATION

Contemporary analysis emphasizes occupational aspects of American Indian gender variance as a central feature. Most frequently a boy's interest in the implements and activities of women and a girl's interest in the tools of male occupations signaled an individual's wish to undertake a gender variant role (Callender and Kochems 1983:447; Whitehead 1981). In hunting societies, for example, female gender variance was signaled by a girl rejecting the domestic activities associated with women and participating in playing and hunting with boys. In the arctic and subarctic, particularly, this was sometimes encouraged by a girl's parents if there were not enough boys to provide the family with food (Lang 1998). Male gender variants were frequently considered especially skilled and industrious in women's crafts and domestic work (though not in agriculture, where this was a man's task) (Roscoe 1991; 1996). Female gender crossers sometimes won reputations as superior hunters and warriors.

Male gender variants' households were often more prosperous than others, sometimes because they were hired by whites. In their own societies the excellence of male gender variants' craftwork was sometimes ascribed to a supernatural sanction for their gender transformation (Callender and Kochems 1983:448). Female gender variants opted out of motherhood, so were not encumbered by caring for children, which may explain their success as hunters or warriors. In some societies, gender

Finds Them and Kills Them,
a Crow Indian gender variant, widely known as a superior warrior (National
Anthropological Archives,
Smithsonian Institution,
photo no. 88-135.)

variants could engage in both men's and women's work, and this, too,
accounted for their increased wealth. Another source of income was payment for the special social activities of gender variants due to their intermediate gender status, such as acting as go-betweens in marriage.
Through their diverse occupations, then, gender variants were often central rather than marginal in their societies.

Early anthropological explanations of male gender variant roles as
a niche for a "failed" or cowardly man who wished to avoid warfare or
other aspects of the masculine role are no longer widely accepted. To
begin with, masculinity was not associated with warrior status in all
American Indian cultures. In some societies, male gender variants were
warriors and in many others, males who rejected the warrior role did not
become gender variants. Sometimes male gender variants did not go to
war because of cultural prohibitions against their using symbols of maleness, for example, the prohibition against their using the bow among the
Illinois. Where male gender variants did not fight, they sometimes had
other important roles in warfare, like treating the wounded, carrying
supplies for the war party, or directing postbattle ceremonials (Callender

and Kochems 1983:449). In a few societies male gender variants became outstanding warriors, such as Finds Them and Kills Them, a Crow Indian who performed daring feats of bravery while fighting with the United States Army against the Crow's traditional enemies, the Lakota Sioux (Roscoe 1998:23).

GENDER VARIANCE AND SEXUALITY

Generally, sexuality was not central in defining gender status among American Indians. But in any case, the assumption by European observers that gender variants were homosexuals meant they did not take much trouble to investigate or record information on this topic. In some American Indian societies same-sex sexual desire/practice did figure significantly in the definition of gender variant roles; in others it did not (Callender and Kochems 1983:449). Some early reports noted specifically that male gender variants lived with and/or had sexual relations with women as well as men; in other societies they were reported as having sexual relations only with men, and in still other societies, of having no sexual relationships at all (Lang 1998:189–95).

The bisexual orientation of some gender variant persons may have been a culturally accepted expression of their gender variance. It may have resulted from an individual's life experiences, such as the age at which he or she entered the gender variant role, and/or it may have been one aspect of the general freedom of sexual expression in many American Indian societies. While male and female gender variants most frequently had sexual relations with, or married, persons of the same biological sex as themselves, these relationships were not considered homosexual in the contemporary Western understanding of that term. In a multiple gender system the partners would be of the same sex but different genders, and homogender, rather than homosexual, practices bore the brunt of negative cultural sanctions. The sexual partners of gender variants were never considered gender variants themselves.

The Navajo are a good example (Thomas 1997). The Navajo have four genders; in addition to man and woman there are two gender variants: masculine female-bodied nádleeh and feminine male-bodied nádleeh. A sexual relationship between a female nádleeh and a woman or a sexual relationship between a male-bodied nádleeh and a man were not stigmatized because these persons were of different genders, although of the same biological sex. However, a sexual relationship between two women, two men, two female-bodied nádleeh or two male-bodied nádleeh, was considered homosexual, and even incestual, and was strongly disapproved of.

The relation of sexuality to variant sex/gender roles across North America suggests that sexual relations between gender variants and persons of the same biological sex were a result rather than a cause of gender variance. Sexual relationships between a man and a male gender variant were accepted in most American Indian societies, though not in all, and appear to have been negatively sanctioned only when it interfered with child-producing heterosexual marriages. Gender variants' sexual relationships varied from casual and wide-ranging (Europeans used the term promiscuous), to stable, and sometimes even involved life-long marriages. In some societies, however, male gender variants were not permitted to engage in long-term relationships with men, either in or out of wedlock. In many cases, gender variants were reported as living alone.

There are some practical reasons why a man might desire sexual relations with a (male) gender variant: in some societies taboos on sexual relations with menstruating or pregnant women restricted opportunities for sexual intercourse; in other societies, sexual relations with a gender variant person were exempt from punishment for extramarital affairs; in still other societies, for example, among the Navajo, some gender variants were considered especially lucky and a man might hope to vicariously partake of this quality by having sexual relations with them (Lang 1998:349).

BIOLOGICAL SEX AND GENDER TRANSFORMATIONS

European observers often confused gender variants with hermaphrodites. Some American Indian societies explicitly distinguished hermaphrodites from gender variants and treated them differently; others assigned gender variant persons and hermaphrodites to the same alternative gender status. With the exception of the Navajo, in most American Indian societies biological sex (or the intersexedness of the hermaphrodite) was not the criterion for a gender variant role, nor were the individuals who occupied gender variant roles anatomically abnormal. The Navajo distinguished between the intersexed and the alternatively gendered, but treated them similarly, though not exactly the same (Thomas 1997; Hill 1935).

And even as the traditional Navajo sex/gender system had biological sex as its starting point, it was only a starting point, and Navajo nádleeh were distinguished by sex-linked behaviors, such as body language, clothing, ceremonial roles, speech style, and work. Feminine, male bodied nádleeh might engage in women's activities such as cooking, weaving, household tasks, and making pottery. Masculine, female-bodied nádleeh, unlike other female-bodied persons, avoided childbirth;

today they are associated with male occupational roles such as construction or firefighting (although ordinary women also sometimes engage in these occupations). Traditionally, female-bodied nádleeh had specific roles in Navajo ceremonials (Thomas 1997).

Thus, even where hermaphrodites occupied a special gender variant role, American Indian gender variance was defined more by cultural than biological criteria. In one recorded case of an interview with and physical examination of a gender variant male, the previously mentioned Finds Them and Kills Them, his genitals were found to be completely normal (Roscoe 1998).

If American Indian gender variants were not generally hermaphrodites, or conceptualized as such, neither were they conceptualized as transsexuals. Gender transformations among gender variants were recognized as only a partial transformation, and the gender variant was not thought of as having become a person of the opposite sex/gender. Rather, gender variant roles were autonomous gender roles that combined the characteristics of men and women and had some unique features of their own. This was sometimes symbolically recognized: among the Zuni a male gender variant was buried in women's dress but men's trousers on the men's side of the graveyard (Parsons quoted in Callender and Kochems 1983:454; Roscoe 1991:124, 145). Male gender variants were neither men—by virtue of their chosen occupations, dress, demeanor, and possibly sexuality—nor women, because of their anatomy and their inability to bear children. Only among the Mohave do we find the extreme imitation of women's physiological processes related to reproduction and the claims to have female sexual organs—both of which were ridiculed within Mohave society. But even here, where informants reported that female gender variants did not menstruate, this did not make them culturally men. Rather it was the mixed quality of gender variant status that was culturally elaborated in native North America, and this was the source of supernatural powers sometimes attributed to them.

SACRED POWER

The association between the spiritual power and gender variance occurred in most, if not all, Native American societies. Even where, as previously noted, recruitment to the role was occasioned by a child's interest in occupational activities of the opposite sex, supernatural sanction, frequently appearing in visions or dreams, was also involved. Where this occurred, as it did mainly in the Prairie and Plains societies, the visions involved female supernatural figures, often the moon. Among the Omaha, for example, the moon appeared in a dream holding a burden strap—a symbol of female work—in one hand, and a bow—a symbol of male work—in the other. When the male dreamer reached for the bow, the moon forced him to take the burden strap (Whitehead 1981). Among the Mohave, a child's choice of male or female implements heralding gender variant status was sometimes prefigured by a dream that was believed to come to an embryo in the womb (Devereux 1937).

Sometimes, by virtue of the power associated with their gender ambiguity, gender variants were ritual adepts and curers, or had special ritual functions (Callender and Kochems 1983:453, Lang 1998). Gender variants did not always have important sacred roles in native North America, however. Where feminine qualities were associated with these roles, male gender variants might become spiritual leaders or healers, but where these roles were associated with male qualities they were not entered into by male gender variants. Among the Plains Indians, with their emphasis on the vision as a source of supernatural power, male gender variants were regarded as holy persons, but in California Indian societies, this was not the case and in some American Indian societies gender variants were specifically excluded from religious roles (Lang 1998:167). Sometimes it was the individual personality of the gender variant rather than his/her gender variance itself, that resulted in occupying sacred roles (see Commentary following Callender and Kochems 1983). Nevertheless, the importance of sacred power was so widely associated with sex/gender diversity in native North America that it is generally agreed to be an important explanation of the frequency of gender diversity in this region of the world.

In spite of cultural differences, some significant similarities among American Indian societies are particularly consistent with multigender systems and the positive value placed on sex/gender diversity (Lang 1996). One of these similarities is a cosmology (system of religious beliefs and way of seeing the world) in which transformation and ambiguity are recurring themes. Thus a person who contains both masculine and feminine qualities or one who is transformed from the sex/gender assigned at birth into a different gender in later life manifests some of the many kinds of transformations and ambiguities that are possible, not only for humans, but for animals and objects in the natural environment. Indeed, in many American Indian cultures, sex/gender ambiguity, lack of sexual differentiation, and sex/gender transformations play an important part in the story of creation (Lang 1996:187). American Indian cosmology may not be "the cause" of sex/gender diversity but it certainly (as in India) provides a hospitable context for it.

THE ALYHA: A MALE GENDER VARIANT ROLE AMONG THE MOHAVE

One of the most complete classic anthropological descriptions of a gender variant role is from the Mohave, a society that lives in the southwest desert area of the Nevada/California border. The following description, based on interviews by anthropologist George Devereux (1937) with some old informants who remembered the transvestite ceremony and had heard stories about gender variant individuals from their elders, indicates some of the ways in which gender variance functioned in native North America.

The Mohave had two gender variant roles: a male role called alyha and a female role called *hwame.* In this society, pregnant women had dreams forecasting the anatomic sex of their children. Mothers of a future alyha dreamt of male characteristics, such as arrow feathers, indicating the birth of a boy, but their dreams also included hints of their child's future gender variant status. A boy indicated he might become an alyha by "acting strangely" around the age of 10 or 11, before he had participated in the boys' puberty ceremonies. At this age, young people began to engage seriously in the activities that would characterize their adult lives as men and women; boys, for example, learned to hunt, ride horses, make bows and arrows, and they developed sexual feelings for girls. The future alyha avoided these masculine activities. Instead he played with dolls, imitated the domestic work of women, tried to participate in the women's gambling games, and demanded to wear the female bark skirt rather than the male breechclout.

The alyha's parents and relatives were ambivalent about this behavior. At first his parents would try to dissuade him, but if the behavior persisted his relatives would resign themselves and begin preparations for the transvestite ceremony. The ceremony was meant to take the boy by surprise; it was considered both a test of his inclination and an initiation. Word was sent out to various settlements so that people could watch the ceremony and get accustomed to the boy in female clothing. At the ceremony, the boy was led into a circle of onlookers by two women, and the crowd began singing the transvestite songs. If the boy began to dance as women did, he was confirmed as an alyha. He was then taken to the river to bathe and given a girl's skirt to wear. This initiation ceremony confirmed his changed gender status, which was considered permanent.

After this ceremony the alyha assumed a female name (though he did not take the lineage name that all females assumed) and would resent being called by his former, male name. In the frequent and bawdy sexual joking characteristic of Mohave culture, an alyha resented male nomenclature being applied to his genitals. He insisted that his penis be

called a clitoris, his testes, labia majora, and anus a vagina. Alyha were
also particularly sensitive to sexual joking, and if they were teased in the
same way as women they responded with assaults on those who teased
them. Because they were very strong, people usually avoided angering
them.

Alyha were considered highly industrious and much better house-
wives than were young girls. It is partly for this reason that they had no
difficulty finding spouses, and alyha generally had husbands. Alyha
were not courted like ordinary girls, however (where the prospective husband would sleep chastely beside the girl for several nights and then lead
her out of her parents' house), but rather courted like widows, divorcees,
or "wanton" women. Intercourse with an alyha was surrounded by special etiquette. Like Mohave heterosexual couples, the alyha and her husband practiced both anal and oral intercourse, with the alyha taking the
female role. Alyha were reported to be embarrassed by an erection and
would not allow their sexual partners to touch or even comment on their
erect penis.

When an alyha found a husband, she would begin to imitate menstruation by scratching herself between the legs with a stick until blood
appeared. The alyha then submitted to puberty observations as a girl
would, and her husband also observed the requirements of the husband
of a girl who menstruated for the first time. Alyha also imitated pregnancy, particularly if their husbands threatened them with divorce on the
grounds of barrenness. At this time they would cease faking menstruation and follow the pregnancy taboos, with even more attention than ordinary women, except that they publicly proclaimed their pregnancy, which
ordinary Mohave women never did. In imitating pregnancy, an alyha
would stuff rags in her skirts, and near the time of the birth, drank a
decoction to cause constipation. After a day or two of stomach pains, she
would go into the bushes and sit over a hole, defecating in the position of
childbirth. The feces would be treated as a stillbirth and buried, and the
alyha would weep and wail as a woman does for a stillborn child. The
alyha and her husband would then clip their hair as in mourning.

Alyha were said to be generally peaceful persons, except when
teased, and were also considered to be cowards. They did not have to participate in the frequent and harsh military raids of Mohave men. Alyha
did participate in the welcoming home feast for the warriors, where, like
old women, they might make a bark penis and go through the crowd pok-
ing the men who had stayed home, saying, "You are not a man, but an
alyha."

In general, alyha were not teased or ridiculed for being alyha
(though their husbands were teased for marrying them), because it was
believed that they could not help it and that a child's inclinations in this
direction could not be resisted. It was believed that a future alyha's

desire for a gender change was such that he could not resist dancing the women's dance at the initiation ceremony. Once his desires were demonstrated in this manner, people would not thwart him. It was partly the belief that becoming an alyha was a result of a "temperamental compulsion" or predestined (as forecast in his mother's pregnancy dream) that inhibited ordinary Mohave from ridiculing alyha. In addition, alyha were considered powerful healers, especially effective in curing sexually transmitted diseases (also called alyha) like syphilis.

The alyha demonstrates some of the ways in which gender variant roles were constructed as autonomous genders in North America. In many ways the alyha crossed genders, but the role had a distinct, alternative status to that of both man and woman (as did the hwame). Although the alyha imitated many aspects of a woman's role—dress, sexual behavior, menstruation, pregnancy, childbirth, and domestic occupations—they were also recognized as being different from women. Alyha did not take women's lineage names; they were not courted like ordinary women; they publicly proclaimed their pregnancies; and they were considered more industrious than other women in women's domestic tasks.

In spite of the alyha's sexual relations with men, the alyha was not considered primarily a homosexual (in Western terms). In fact, among ordinary Mohave, if a person dreamed of having homosexual relationships, that person would be expected to die soon, but this was not true of the alyha. Most significantly, the alyha were believed to have special supernatural powers, which they used in curing illness.

FEMALE GENDER VARIANTS

Female gender variants probably occurred more frequently among American Indians than in other cultures, although this has been largely overlooked in the historic and ethnographic record (But see Blackwood 1984; Jacobs et al. 1997; Lang 1998; Medicine 1983).

Although the generally egalitarian social structures of many American Indian societies provided a hospitable context for female gender variance, it occurred in perhaps only one-quarter to one-half of the societies with male variant roles (Callender and Kochems 1983:446; see also Lang 1998:262–65). This may be explained partly by the fact that in many American Indian societies women could—and did—adopt aspects of the male gender role, such as warfare or hunting, and sometimes dressed in male clothing, without being reclassified into a different gender (Blackwood 1984; Lang 1998:261ff; Medicine 1983).

As with males, the primary criteria of changed gender status for females was an affinity for the occupations of the other gender. While this inclination for male occupations was often displayed in childhood, female gender variants entered these roles later in life than did males (Lang 1998:303). Among some Inuit, "men pretenders" would refuse to learn women's tasks and were taught male occupations when they were children, by their fathers. They played with boys and participated in the hunt. Among the Kaska, a family who had only daughters might select one to "be like a man"; by engaging in the male activity of hunting, she would help provide the family with food. Among the Mohave, too, hwame refused to learn women's work, played with boys, and were considered excellent providers, as well as particularly efficient healers (Blackwood 1984:30; Lang 1998:286). Among the Cheyenne, the *hetaneman* (defined as a hermaphrodite having more of the female element) were great female warriors who accompanied the male warrior societies into battle. In all other groups, however, even outstanding women warriors were not recast into a different gender role (Roscoe 1998:75). Female gender variants also sometimes entered specialized occupations, becoming traders, guides for whites, or healers. The female preference for male occupations might be motivated by a female's desire to be independent, or might be initiated or encouraged by a child's parents, and in some societies was sanctioned through supernatural omens or in dreams.

In addition to occupation, female gender variants might assume other characteristics of men. Cocopa *warrhameh* wore a masculine hairstyle and had their noses pierced, like boys (Lang 1998:283). Among the Maidu, the female *suku* also had her nose pierced on the occasion of her initiation into the men's secret society. Mohave hwame were tattooed like men instead of women. Transvestism was commonly though not universally practiced: it occurred, for example, among the Kaska, Paiute, Ute, and Mohave.

Like male gender variants, female gender variants exhibited a wide range of sexual relationships. Some had relationships with other females, who were generally regarded as ordinary women. Only rarely, as among a southern Apache group, was the female gender variant (like her male counterpart) defined in terms of her sexual desire for women. Mohave hwame engaged in sexual and marriage relationships with women, although they courted them in a special way, different from heterosexual courtships. If a hwame married a pregnant woman, she could claim paternity of the child, although the child belonged to the descent group of its biological father (Devereux 1937:514). Like an alyha's husband, a hwame's wife was often teased, and hwame marriages were generally unstable. Masahai Amatkwisai, the most well known hwame, married women three times and was also known to have sexual relationships with many men. Masahai's wives were all aggressively teased by male Mohave who viewed "real" sexual relations only in terms of penetration by a penis. At dances Masahai sat with the men, described her wife's genitals, and flirted with girls, all typical male behavior. Masahai's masculine behavior was ridiculed, and the men gravely insulted her (though never to her face), by referring to her by an obscene nickname meaning the female genitals. The harassment of Masahai's wives apparently led to the eventual breakup of her marriages.

Sexual relationships between women in American Indian societies were rarely historically documented, but in any case, were generally downplayed in female gender variant roles, even when this involved marriage. One female gender variant, for example, Woman Chief, a famous Crow warrior and hunter, took four wives, but this appeared to be primarily an economic strategy: processing animal hides among the Crow was women's work, so that Woman Chief's polygyny (multiple spouses) complemented her hunting skills.

While most often American Indian women who crossed genders occupationally, such as Woman Chief, were not reclassified into a gender variant role, several isolated cases of female gender transformations have been documented historically. One of these is Ququnak Patke, a "manlike woman" from the Kutenai (Schaeffer 1965). Ququnak Patke had married a white fur trader and when she returned to her tribe, claimed that her husband had transformed her into a man. She wore men's clothes, lived as a man, married a woman and claimed supernatural sanction for her role change and her supernatural powers. Although whites often mistook her for a man in her various roles as warrior, explorer's guide, and trader, such transformations were not considered a possibility among the Kutenai, and many thought Ququnak Patke was mad. She died attempting to mediate a quarrel between two hostile Indian groups.

It is difficult to know how far we can generalize about the relation of sexuality to female gender variance in precontact American Indian cultures from the lives of the few documented female gender variants. These descriptions (and those for males, as well) are mainly based on ethnographic accounts that relied on twentieth-century informants whose memories were already shaped by white hostility toward gender diversity and same-sex sexuality. Nevertheless, it seems clear that although American Indian female gender variants clearly had sexual relationships with women, sexual object choice was not their defining characteristic. In some cases, female gender variants were described "as women who never marry," which does not say anything definitive about their sexuality; it may well be that the sexuality of female gender variants was more variable than that of men.

Occasionally, as with Masahai and Ququnak Patke, and also for some male gender variants, contact with whites opened up opportunities for gender divergent individuals (see Roscoe 1988; 1991). On the whole, however, as a result of Euro-American repression and the growing assimilation of Euro-American sex/gender ideologies, both female and male gender variant roles among American Indians largely disappeared by the 1930s, as the reservation system was well under way. And yet, its echoes may remain. The current academic interest in American Indian multigender roles, and particularly the testimony of contemporary two-spirits, remind us that alternatives are possible and that understanding American Indian sex/gender diversity in the past and present makes a significant contribution to understandings of sex/gender diversity in the larger society.

Chapter Two

Hijra and Sādhin
Neither Man nor Woman in India

As in native North America, gender diversity in Hindu India is mainly set within a religious context. Unlike North America, however, gender diversity in India is set within a basically binary sex/gender system that is hierarchical and patriarchal rather than one that is egalitarian.

In Hindu India, male and female/man and woman are viewed as natural categories in complementary opposition. This binary construction incorporates—and conflates—biological qualities (sex) and cultural qualities (gender). Males and females are born with different sexual characteristics and reproductive organs, have different sexual natures, and take different and complementary roles in marriage, sexual behavior, and reproduction. The biological or "essential" nature of the differences between male and female, man and woman, is amply demonstrated in the medical and ritual texts of classical Hinduism, in which body fluids and sexual organs are presented as both the major sources of the sex/gender dichotomy and its major symbols (O'Flaherty 1980).

In Hinduism, in contrast to Western culture, the female principle is the more active, animating the male principle, which is more inert and latent. This active female principle has an erotic, creative, life-giving aspect and a destructive, life-destroying aspect. The erotic aspect of female power is dangerous unless it is controlled by the male principle. Powerful women, whether deities or humans, must be restrained by male authority. Thus, the Hindu Mother Goddess is kind and helpful when subordinated to her male consort, but when dominant, the goddess is aggressive, devouring, and destructive. The view that unrestrained female sexuality is dangerous characterizes a more down-to-earth sexual ideology as well. In India, both in Hinduism and in Islam, women are believed to be more sexually voracious than men; in order to prevent their sexual appetites from causing social chaos and distracting men from their higher spiritual duties, women must be controlled.

THE RELIGIOUS CONTEXT OF GENDER DIVERSITY

The most important context for understanding sex/gender diversity in Indian society is Hindu religious concepts (Nanda 1999). In Hinduism, in spite of the importance of the basic complementary opposition of male and female, many sex/gender variants and transformations are also acknowledged. Unlike Western cultures and religions, which try to resolve, repress, or dismiss sexual contradictions and ambiguities as jokes or trivia, Hinduism has a great capacity to allow opposites to confront each other without necessarily resolving the opposition, "celebrating the idea that the universe is boundlessly various, and . . . that all possibilities may exist without excluding each other" (O'Flaherty 1973:318). The presence of alternative genders and gender transformations in Hinduism gives positive meaning to the lives of many individuals with a variety of alternative gender identifications, physical conditions, and erotic preferences. Despite the criminalization of many kinds of transgender behavior under British rule and even by the Indian government after independence, Indian society has not yet permitted cultural anxiety about transgenderism to express itself in culturally institutionalized phobias and repressions.

Ancient Hindu origin myths often feature androgynous or hermaphroditic ancestors. The Rg Veda (a classical Hindu religious text), for example, says that before creation the world lacked all distinctions, including those of sex and gender. Ancient poets often expressed this concept with androgynous or hermaphroditic images, such as a male with a womb, a male deity with breasts, or a pregnant male (Zwilling and Sweet 2000:101). In Hinduism, then, multiple sexes and genders are acknowledged as possibilities, albeit ambivalently regarded possibilities, both among humans and deities. Individuals who do not fit into society's major sex/gender categories may be stigmatized but may also find, within Hinduism, meaningful and valued gender identifications.

Hinduism has been characterized as having a "propensity towards androgynous thinking" (Zwilling and Sweet 2000:100). Within the Hindu sex/gender system, the interchange of male and female qualities, transformations of sex and gender, the incorporation of male and female within one person, and alternative sex and gender roles among deities and humans are meaningful and positive themes in mythology, ritual and art. Among the many kinds of male and female sex/gender variants, the most visible and culturally institutionalized are the *hijras*.

Hijras are culturally defined as "neither man nor woman." They are born as males and through a ritual surgical transformation become an alternative, third sex/gender category (Nanda 1999). Hijras worship Bahuchara Mata, a form of the Hindu Mother Goddess particularly associated with transgenderism. Their traditional employment is to perform at marriages and after a child (especially a son) has been born. They sing and dance and bless the child and the family for increased fertility and prosperity in the name of the goddess. They then receive traditional payments of money, sweets, and cloth in return.

HIJRAS AS NOT-MEN . . .

The recognition of more than two sex/genders is recorded in India as early as the eighth century BCE; like the hijras, alternative or third sex/gendered persons were primarily considered to be defective males. The core of their deficiency centered on their sexual impotence, or inability to procreate (Zwilling and Sweet 1996:361). In India today, the term hijra is most commonly translated as "eunuch" or intersexed, and emphasizes sexual impotence. Hijras are culturally defined as persons who are born as males but who adopt the clothing, behavior and occupations of women, and who are neither male nor female, neither man nor woman.

Hijra sexual impotence is popularly understood as a *physical* defect impairing the male sexual function in intercourse (in the inserter role) and in reproduction. This is the major way in which hijras are "not-men." Hijras attribute their impotence to a defective male sexual organ. A child who at birth is classified as male but whose genitals are subsequently noticed to be ambiguous, culturally would be defined as a hijra, or as potentially a hijra (though in fact not all such individuals become hijras).

Like their counterparts in native North America, hijras (as receptors) frequently have sexual relationships with men. While hijras are not defined by their sexual practices, they often define themselves as "men who have no desire for women." Linguistically and culturally, hijras are distinguished from other men who take the receptor role in sex and are identified by their same-sex sexual orientation (Cohen 1995). It is the hijras' sexual impotence and in-between sex/gender status that is at the core of their cultural definition. A male who is not biologically intersexed who wishes to become a hijra must transform his sex/gender through the emasculation operation (discussed later in this chapter).

Although all hijras explain their deficient masculinity by saying, "I was born this way," this statement is not factually true. Rather, it expresses the Hindu view that qualities of both sex and gender are inborn, and is also consistent with the Hindu view that fate is important in shaping one's life chances and experiences.

HIJRAS AS WOMEN AND NOT-WOMEN

While hijras are "man minus man," they are also "man plus woman." Hijras adopt many aspects of the feminine gender role. They wear women's dress, hairstyle, and accessories; they imitate women's walk, gestures, voice, facial expressions and language; they have only male sexual partners and they experience themselves positively as sexual objects of men's desires. Hijras take feminine names as part of their gender transformation and use female kinship terms for many of their relationships with each other, such as sister, aunty, and grandmother (Hall 1995). They request "ladies only" seating in public transportation and they periodically demand to be counted as women (rather than men) in the census. Being a hijra means not only divesting oneself of one's masculine identity, but also taking on a feminine one.

Although hijras are "like" women, they are also "not-women." Their feminine dress and manners are often exaggerations and their aggressive female sexuality contrasts strongly with the normatively submissive demeanor of ordinary women. Hijra performances do not attempt a realistic imitation of women but rather a burlesque, and the very act of dancing in public violates norms of feminine behavior. Hijras also use coarse and abusive speech, both among themselves and to their audiences, which is also deviant for Indian women. Hijras' use of verbal insult is an important component in the construction of their gender variance, as noted by early European observers and the contemporary Indian media (Hall 1997).

Because hijras are defined as neither men nor women they were sometimes prohibited from wearing women's clothing exclusively: some Indian rulers in the eighteenth century required that hijras distinguish themselves by wearing a man's turban with their female clothing. A century later, hijras were reported as wearing "a medley of male and female clothing," with a female sari under a male coat-like, outer garment (Preston 1987:373). This seems similar to North American gender variant transvestism, though hijras today for the most part do not wear gender-mixed clothing.

The major reason why hijras are considered—by themselves and others—as not-woman is that they do not have female reproductive organs and therefore cannot have children. The hijras tell a story about a hijra who prayed to god to bear a child. God granted her wish, but since she had not specifically prayed for the child to be born, she could not give birth. She remained pregnant until she could not stand the weight any more and slit her stomach open to deliver the baby. Both the hijra and the baby died. This story illustrates that it is against the nature of hijras to reproduce like women do, thereby denying them full identification as women.

RELIGIOUS IDENTIFICATIONS

An important sex/gender identification of hijras is with Arjun, hero of the great Hindu epic, the Mahabharata. In one episode Arjun is exiled and lives for a year in the disguise of a eunuch-transvestite, wearing women's dress and bracelets, braiding his hair like a woman, and teaching singing and dancing to the women of the king's court. In this role he also participates in weddings and childbirths, a clear point of identification with the hijras (Hiltelbeitel 1980).

The hijras' identification with Arjun is visually reinforced by Arjun's representation in popular drama as a vertically divided half-man/half-woman. In this form Arjun is identified with the sexually ambivalent deity, Shiva, who is also frequently represented as a vertically divided half-man/half-woman, symbolizing his union with his female energy.

Shiva is particularly associated with the concept of creative asceticism, which is the core of hijra identity and power. In Hinduism, sexual impotence can be transformed into procreative power through the practice of asceticism, or the renunciation of sex. The power that results from sexual abstinence (called *tapas)* paradoxically becomes an essential feature in the process of creation.

In one Hindu creation myth, Shiva was asked to create the world, but took so long to do so that the power of creation was given to another deity, Brahma (The Creator). When Shiva was finally ready to begin creation he saw that the universe was already created and got so angry, he broke off his phallus saying "there is no use for this," and threw it into the earth. Paradoxically, as soon as Shiva's phallus ceased to be a source of individual fertility, it became a source of universal fertility (O'Flaherty 1973). This paradox expresses the power of the hijras who as emasculated men are individually impotent but nevertheless are able to confer blessings for fertility on others. As creative ascetics hijras are considered auspicious and powerful, and this underlies their ritual performances at marriages and childbirth.

While at one level the hijras' claim to power is through Shiva's ritual sacrifice of the phallus, at a more conscious and culturally elaborated level, the power of the hijras is based on their identification with the Mother Goddess. In Hindu India, salvation and success are equated with submission, particularly in regard to the Mother Goddess. The Mother

Goddess must offer help when confronted with complete surrender of the devotee, but those who deny her wishes put themselves in danger. Thus, underlying the surrender is fear. The protective and destructive aspects of the Mother Goddess, expressed in myth and ritual, represent the ambivalence toward the real mother that is perhaps universal. But the Hindu Mother Goddess is singularly intense in her destructive aspects, which, nevertheless, contain the seeds of salvation (for a comparison of female goddesses with eunuch priests, see Roller 1999). Popular Hindu mythology (and its hijra versions) abounds in images of the aggressive Mother Goddess as she devours, beheads, and castrates—destructive acts that nevertheless contain the possibility of rebirth, as in the hijra emasculation ritual. This dual nature of the goddess provides the powerful symbolic and psychological context in which the hijras become culturally meaningful as an alternative sex/gender.

Bahuchara Mata, a version of the Mother Goddess, is the special object of devotion for the hijras. (Photograph by Serena Nanda.)

Deficient masculinity by itself does not make a hijra. Hijras are deficient men who receive a call from their goddess—which they ignore at the peril of being born impotent for seven future rebirths—to undergo a sex and gender change, wear their hair long, and dress in women's clothes. The sex change, which involves surgical removal of the genitals, is called "the operation" (even by hijras who do not otherwise speak English). For hijras, the operation is a form of rebirth and it contains many of the symbolic elements of childbirth. Only after the operation do hijras become vehicles of the power of the Mother Goddess whose blessings they bestow at weddings and childbirth. For hijras not born intersexed, the operation transforms an impotent, "useless" male into a hijra, and a vehicle of the procreative power of the Mother Goddess.

The operation is explicitly identified with the hijras' devotion to Bahuchara Mata, who is particularly associated with male transvestism and transgenderism. Several hijras are always present at Bahuchara's temple, near Ahmedabad, in Gujerat, to bless visitors and tell them about the power of the goddess.

The surgery is (ideally) performed by a hijra, called a "midwife." The client is seated in front of a picture of the goddess and repeats Bahuchara's name over and over, which induces a trancelike state. The midwife then severs all or part of the genitals (penis and testicles) from the body with two diagonal cuts with a sharp knife. The blood from the operation, which is considered part of the male identity, is allowed to flow freely; this rids the person of their maleness. The resulting wound is healed by traditional medical practices and a small hole is left open for urination. After the operation the new hijra is subject to many of the same restrictions as a woman after childbirth and is supervised and taken care of by hijra elders. In the final stage of the ritual, the hijra is dressed as a bride, signifying the active sexuality potential in marriage, and is taken through the streets in procession. This completes the ritual and the sex/gender transformation. Although emasculation is prohibited by Indian law, hijras continue to practice it secretly (Ranade 1983).

HIJRAS AS ASCETICS

In India, gender is an important part of being a full social person. Through marriage, men and women are expected to produce children, especially sons, in order to continue the family line. An individual who dies without being married, an impotent man, or a woman who does not menstruate is considered an incomplete person. However, the individual who is not capable of reproduction, as either a man or a woman, or who does not wish to marry, is not necessarily excluded from society (see female gender variants later in this chapter). In India, a meaningful role that transcends the categories of (married) man and (married) woman is that of the ascetic, or renouncer, a person both outside society yet also part of it. In identifying with the ascetic role, individuals who are sexually "betwixt and between" for any number of biological reasons or personal choices are able to transform an incomplete personhood into a transcendent one. Within the Hindu religion, the life path of an ascetic is one of the many diverse paths that an individual may take to achieve salvation.

Hijras identify themselves as ascetics in their renunciation of sexual desire, in abandoning their family and kinship ties, and in their dependence on alms (religiously inspired charity) for their livelihood. As ascetics, hijras transcend the stigma of their sex/gender deficiencies.

An important Hindu belief, called **dharma**, is that every individual has a life path of his/her own that he/she must follow, because every individual has different innate essences, moral qualities, and special abilities. This leads to an acceptance of many different occupations, behaviors, and personal styles as legitimate life paths. This is particularly so when the behavior is sanctified by tradition, formalized in ritual, and practiced within a group (Kakar 1982:163). Hinduism thus affords the individual personality wide latitude in behavior, including that which Euro-American cultures might label criminal or pathological and attempt to punish or cure. This Hindu concept of the legitimacy of many different life paths applies to hijras and to other sex/gender variants as well.

RITUAL ROLES AND SOCIAL ACCEPTANCE

In India, the birth of a son is viewed as a major purpose of marriage. As auspicious and powerful ritual figures, on this occasion hijras bless the child and the family and provide entertainment for friends, relatives, and neighbors. These hijra performances, which include folk and current film songs and dances, also have comic aspects. These mainly derive from the hijras' burlesque of women's behavior, especially aggressive sexuality, and mimicking the pains of pregnancy at each month.

At some point in the performance, one hijra inspects the genitals of the newborn to ascertain its sex. Hijras claim that any baby born intersexed belongs to their community and it is widely believed in India that this claim cannot be resisted. The hijras then confer the power of the Mother Goddess to bless the child for what they themselves do not possess—the power of creating new life, of having many sons, and of carrying on the continuity of a family line. When the performance is completed, the hijras claim their traditional payment.

As part of their traditional ritual performance role when a son is born, hijras examine the baby's genitals to confirm his sex. (Photograph by Serena Nanda.)

Hijras also perform after a marriage, when the new bride has come to her husband's home (traditionally, and even today ideally, the couple lives with the groom's parents). The hijras bless the couple so that they will have many sons, which is not only the desire of the family, but also means more work for the hijras. These performances contain flamboyant sexual displays and references to sexuality, which break all the rules of normal social intercourse in gender-mixed company and on this occasion are a source of humor. The hijras' skits and songs refer to potentially conflicting relationships in Indian marriages, for example between mother-in-law and daughter-in-law, or between sisters-in-law. As outsiders to the social structure because of their ambiguous sex/gender status, the hijras are uniquely able to expose the points of tension in a culture where sex, gender, and reproduction are involved. In humorously expressing this tension, the hijras defuse it, yet at the same time, their very ambiguity of sex and gender keep the tension surrounding sex, gender, and fertility alive.

Hijras are generally regarded with ambivalence; social attitudes include a combination of mockery, fear, respect, contempt, and even compassion. Fear of the hijras is related to the "virility complex" in India, which has an ancient history and which is also part of contemporary culture. This complex identifies manhood with semen and sexual potency, both of central concern in India's patriarchal culture (Zwilling and Sweet n.d.:6). Hijras have the power to curse as well as to bless, and if they are not paid their due, they will insult a family publicly and curse it with a loss of virility. The ultimate weapon of a hijra is to raise her skirt and display her mutilated genitals; this is both a source of shame and a contamination of the family's reproductive potential.

Hijras are also feared for another reason. Having renounced normal family life, hijras are outside the social roles and relationships of caste and kinship, which define the social person in Hindu culture and which are the main sources of social control of an individual (Ostor, Fruzzetti, and Barnett 1982). Hijras (and other ascetics) are thus an implicit threat to the social order (Lannoy 1975; O'Flaherty 1973). The hijras use their sexual and social marginality to manipulate and exploit the public to their own advantage. Hijras themselves say that because they are marginal to the social rules that govern the behavior of men and women, they are a people without "shame" (Hall 1995; 1997:445). Hijra audiences know this and feel vulnerable to economic extortion, as they weigh the financial cost of giving in to the hijras' coercive demands for payment against the likelihood that if they do not pay, they will be publicly abused, humiliated, and cursed.

Nevertheless, if hijras challenge their audiences, their audiences also challenge the hijras. Sometimes a member of the hijras' audience will challenge the performers' authenticity by lifting their skirts to see whether they are emasculated and thus "real" hijras or "fake" hijras, men who have male genitals and are thus only impersonating hijras. If hijra performers are found to be "fakes" they are insulted and chased away without payment.

HIJRA SEXUALITY

Part of the ambivalence surrounding hijras focuses on their sexuality. Sexuality is also a source of conflict within the hijra community. As noted above, the term hijra translates as eunuch not homosexual; the power of the hijra role resides in their renunciation of sexuality and the transformation of sexual desire into sacred power. In reality, however, many hijras do engage in sexual activities, exclusively in the receptor role with men and frequently as prostitutes. This is an "open secret" in Indian cities, although known to a different degree among different sections of the population. Sometimes, as in Bombay, hijra prostitutes work out of houses of prostitution located in "red light" districts; in smaller cities and towns they may simply use their own homes to carry on prostitution discretely.

In addition to the exchange of money for sex with a variety of male clients, hijras also have long-term sexual relationships with men they call their "husbands." These relationships may be one-sided and exploitative, as when the "husband" lives off his hijra "wife," but they may also be affectionate and involve some economic reciprocity. Most hijras prefer having a husband to prostitution and many speak of their husbands in very loving terms, as indeed husbands sometimes do of their hijra wives. For many hijras, joining the hijra community provides an opportunity to engage in sexual relations with men in a safer, more organized and orderly environment than is afforded by street prostitution.

Hijra sexual relationships cause conflict within the hijra community, however. Because active sexuality runs counter to the cultural definition of hijras as ascetics, knowledge of hijra prostitution and sexuality undermines their respect in society. In cities where the hijra population is large, hijra prostitutes are not permitted to live with hijra ritual performers. Hijra elders are often jealous of the attachment of individual hijras to their husbands, as this undercuts the economic contribution of a hijra to her household. Some hijras complain that prostitution has increased because the opportunities for ritual performances have declined. In fact, prostitution has been associated with the hijras for hundreds of years, an association that hijras vehemently deny and attribute to those who imitate their effeminacy but who are not "real" hijras.

SOCIAL STRUCTURE OF THE HIJRA COMMUNITY

Indian social structure is built on castes, which are ethnically distinct corporate social units associated with occupational exclusivity, control over their members, and a hierarchically based group allocation of rights and privileges. The Indian caste system includes many different kinds of groups, such as Muslims and tribal peoples, who, though originally outside the Hindu system, were incorporated into it as caste-like groups.

Hijra communities have many caste-like features, which, along with their kinship networks, contribute to their social reproduction (Nanda 1999). Like a caste, the hijra community claims a monopoly over their occupation as ritual performers; exercises control over its members, with outcasting as the ultimate sanction; and rests its legitimacy on origin myths associated with high-status legendary figures like Arjun or deities like Ram or Shiva.

The census of India does not count hijras separately, so estimates of their numbers are unreliable; a common "guesstimate" is 50,000 nation- wide. Hijras predominantly live in the cities of northern India, where they find the greatest opportunity to perform their traditional ritual roles, but small groups of hijras are found all over India, in the south as well as the north, and in rural areas and small towns as well as in big cities.

Hijras are highly organized and participate in a special subculture that extends throughout the nation, with some regional variations. Hijras normally live in households containing between five and twenty members with one elder as a "manager." Each hijra contributes to the running of the household, either with money or by performing domestic tasks. Household composition is flexible, and individuals commonly move from one household to another in a different part of a city or in a different city or region, out of boredom, dissatisfaction, or as the result of a dispute.

The nationwide hijra community is composed of "houses," or named subgroups; houses are not domestic units, but are similar to lineages or clans. Each house recognizes a common "ancestor" and has its own his- tory and special rules. Any particular household contains members of several houses. Each house (not household) has a leader, called a *naik* (chief), and within the major cities, the naiks of the different houses form a kind of executive council, making policy and resolving disputes.

Below the level of the naiks are the gurus. The most significant relationship among hijras is that of *guru* (master, teacher) and *chela* (dis- ciple). An individual is formally initiated into the hijra community under the sponsorship of a guru, who bestows a new female name and pays the initiation fee. The new chela vows to obey her guru and the rules of the house and the community. The guru presents the new chela with some gifts and records her name in the guru's record book. This guru-chela relationship, which replicates the ideals of an extended family, is ideally a lifelong bond of reciprocity in which the guru is obligated to "take care of" and help the chela, while the chela is obligated to be loyal and obedi- ent to the guru. The chela must also give her guru a portion of whatever she earns.

Through the extension of guru-chela relationships, hijras all over India are related by (fictive) kinship (Hall 1995). "Daughters" of one "mother" consider themselves "sisters," and elders are regarded as "grandmothers" or as "mother's sister" (aunt). These relationships involve warm and reciprocal regard and are sometimes formalized by the exchange of small amounts of money, clothing, jewelry, and sweets. In addition to the constant movement of hijras who visit their gurus and fic- tive kin in different cities, religious and secular annual gatherings also bring together thousands of hijras from all over India.

Hijras come from all castes and from Hindu, Muslim and Christian families. Most hijras seem to be from the lower, though not unclean (formerly, untouchable), castes. Within the hijra community, however, all caste affiliations are disregarded and there are no distinctions of purity and pollution. Like other ascetics, hijra identity transcends caste and kinship affiliation.

In pre-independent India, the caste-like status of the hijras was recognized in the princely states, where one hijra in each district was granted hereditary rights to a parcel of land and the right to collect food and small sums of money from each agricultural household in a stipulated area. These rights were protected against other hijras and legitimately inherited within the community. This granting of rights was consistent with the Indian concept of the king's duty to ensure the ancient rights of his subjects (Preston 1987:380). Even today, although in a vague and somewhat confused way, hijras refer back to these rights as part of their claims to legitimacy.

Under British rule in India the hijras lost some of their traditional legitimacy when the British government refused to lend its legal support to the hijras' "right of begging or extorting money, whether authorized by former governments or not." The British thereby hoped to discourage what they found to be "the abominable practices of the wretches." Through a law disallowing any land grant or entitlement from the state to any group that "breach[ed] the laws of public decency," the British finally removed state protection from the hijras (Preston 1987:382). In some British-controlled areas, laws criminalizing emasculation, aimed specifically at the hijras, were enacted. These laws were later incorporated into the criminal code of independent India.

Though emasculation continues, criminalization undercuts social respect for the hijras, particularly when criminal cases are sensationalized in the media. This is also true about the association of hijras with AIDS, though in fact, the spread of AIDS in India is primarily through heterosexual prostitution. In addition, as a result of increasing Westernization of Indian values and culture, at least at a surface level, the role of many traditional ritual performers like the hijras is becoming less compelling. Traditional life-cycle ceremonies are shorter, and expensive and nonessential ritual features are dropping off. In an attempt to compensate for lost earnings, hijras have tried to broaden the definition of occasions on which they claim their performances are necessary, for example, at the birth of a girl as well as a boy or at the opening of a public building or business.

The hijra role incorporates many kinds of contradictions. Hijras are both men and women, yet neither men nor women; their ideal identity is that of chaste ascetics, yet they widely engage in sexual relationships; they are granted the power of the goddess and perform rituals in her name, but they are held in low esteem and are socially marginal. Yet, with all its contradictions and ambiguities, the hijra role continues to be sustained by a culture in which religion still gives positive meaning to gender variance and even accords it a measure of power.

THE SĀDHIN: A FEMALE GENDER VARIANT

Although female gender variants are mentioned in ancient Hindu texts, none are as widespread, visible, or prominent as the hijras. One female gender variant role is the *sādhin* or female ascetic. This role becomes meaningful within the context of Hindu values and culture, particularly regarding the position of women in India (see Humes 1996) and the concept of the ascetic.

As noted above, marriage and reproduction are essential to recognition as a social person in Hindu India, and "spinsters" rarely exist in rural areas. Among the Gaddis, a numerically small pastoral people of the Himalayan foothills, a female gender variant role called sādhin emerged in the late-nineteenth century. Sādhins renounce marriage (and thus, sexuality), though they otherwise live in the material world. They are committed to celibacy for life. Sādhins do not wear women's clothing, but rather the everyday clothing of men, and they wear their hair close cropped (Phillimore 1991).

A girl voluntarily decides to become a sādhin. She usually makes this decision around puberty, before her menarche, though in one reported case, the parents of a six-year-old girl interpreted her preference to dress in boy's clothing and cut her hair like a boy, as an indication of her choice to be a sādhin. For most sādhins, this role choice, which is considered irreversible, is related to their determined rejection of marriage. A sādhin must be a virgin; she is viewed, however, not just as a celibate woman but as a female asexual. Although the transition from pre-sexual child to an asexual sādhin denies a girl's sexual identity, the girl is not considered to have changed her gender, so much as transcended it.

Entering the sādhin role is not marked by ritual, but it is publicly acknowledged when the sādhin adopts men's clothing and has her hair cut in a tonsure, like a boy for his initiation rite into adulthood. Despite her male appearance, however, a sādhin remains socially a woman in many ways, and she retains the female name given to her when she was a child. Sādhins may (but are not obliged to) engage in masculine productive tasks from which women are normally excluded, for example, ploughing, sowing crops, sheep herding, and processing wool. They also, however, do women's work. On gender-segregated ceremonial occasions, adult sādhins may sit with the men as well as smoke the water pipe and cigarettes, definitely masculine behaviors. Yet sādhins do not generally attend funerals, a specifically male prerogative.

Ethnographer Peter Phillimore characterizes the role of the sādhin as an "as if" male (1991:337). A sādhin's gender is not in question, but she can nevertheless operate in many social contexts "like a man." A sādhin can, for example, make the necessary offerings for her father's spirit and the ancestors, a ceremony otherwise performed only by a son. Unlike hijras, though, sādhins have no special ritual or performance roles in society, nor are they considered to have any special sacred powers. Sādhins, like hijras, are ascetics in their renunciation of sexuality, although sādhins are only ambiguous ascetics because they do not renounce other aspects of the material world.

Hindu asceticism is primarily identified with males so that female ascetics behave in significant respects like men; this maleness makes visible and legitimates female asceticism, though it is different from male asceticism in important ways (Humes 1996; Phillimore 1991:341). Unlike male ascetics, who transcend sex/gender classification and who can renounce the world at any age or stage of life, the sādhin's asceticism must begin before puberty and her lifelong chastity, or purity, is essential to the public acceptance of her status. These differences suggest that within orthodox Hinduism, the sādhin role is a way of controlling female sexuality and providing a social niche for the woman who rejects the only legitimate female roles in traditional Hindu India, those of wife and mother.

Because of the importance of women in the subsistence economy, Gaddi society was substantially more gender egalitarian than orthodox Hindus. When Gaddi migration in the late-nineteenth century brought them into contact with more orthodox Hindus, Gaddis came under increasing cultural pressure to curtail the relative equality and freedom of their women. However, because a woman's decision to reject marriage is an unacceptable challenge to gender conventions among the orthodox Hindus, the sādhin role, defined as an asexual female gender variant, acts as a constraint on the potential, unacceptable, sexuality of unmarried women. The definition of the sādhin as asexual transforms "the negative associations of spinsterhood" into the "positive associations of sādhin-hood" (Phillimore 1991:347).

The sādhin role provides one kind of response to the cultural challenge of adult female virginity in a society where marriage and motherhood are the dominant feminine ideals, while the hijra role, despite its many contradictions, gives meaning and even power to male sex/gender ambiguity in a highly patriarchal culture. While all cultures must deal with those whose anatomy or behavior leaves them outside the classification of male and female, man and woman, it is the genius of Hinduism that allows for so many different ways of being human.

Chapter Three

Men and Not-Men
Sexuality and Gender in Brazil

In Brazil sex/gender diversity is associated with the alternative sex/gender roles of ***travesti***, viado, and bicha, most centrally defined by their sexuality, a theme that characterizes most of Latin America (Murray 1995). Underlying cultural variations in the sex/gender ideologies of Latin America is a shared understanding, based on common roots in Spanish and Portuguese culture, of men and women as totally opposed in every way, with males clearly superior (Brandes 1981; Gilmore 1996). This pattern has been central throughout Brazilian history, though today it is one of several sex/gender ideologies that coexist in contradictory, complex and overlapping ways in Brazil.

Brazil's traditional sex/gender system flowered in the early colonial period (sixteenth century) when a plantation slave economy dominated by a class of wealthy landowners was the predominent economic and cultural feature. Plantation landowner patriarchs exercised absolute authority over their dominions, resulting in a rigid social hierarchy of master over (African) slave and men over women. This intersecting class/race/gender hierarchy was sanctioned by official Catholic Church teachings and enforced, when necessary, through violence. Thus, the association of power, domination, and the use or threat of violence became central to Brazilian masculine identity and its system of sexual classification (Parker 1991:31). This traditional sex/gender ideology dominated Brazil throughout the nineteenth and early-twentieth centuries and still retains much of its power today.

The foundation of this system is the dichotomy between man and woman (or rather, as discussed later in this chapter, between man and not-man), masculine and feminine, which are opposed in every way. This opposition is viewed as a natural result of the biological sex differences between males and females. It encompasses many differences—bodies

43

and genitalia, social position, rights and responsibilities, psychological characteristics, sexual desires and capacities, and appropriate spatial and social domains. Men dominate the more important public spheres of political activity and the workplace, while women are acknowledged as superior only in realms regarded as inferior, such as domestic life (Hayes 1996:9).

Power is invested entirely in the hands of men, who are character-ized by their superiority, strength, virility, activity, potential for violence, and legitimate use of force. Masculine virility is manifested in aggressive sexuality and having many children, and also by the ability to control the sexuality of women, that is, daughters and wives.

Women are defined as inferior and weak, yet also beautiful and desirable, and subject always to control by men—fathers and brothers and, after marriage, husbands. A persistent underlying threat to mascu-linity is the loss of control over women. Inherent in the beauty and seduc-tiveness of women is the constant threat of their sexual betrayal, a view that has deep roots in the Christian ideology of women as either virgins, mothers, or whores (Gregg 1997; Parker 1991:49). Virginity is a sign of a woman's innocence and, more importantly, is a demonstration of her proper domination by male authority. Both the prostitute and the unfaithful wife are a deeply felt threat to the system because each in her own way escapes the control of legitimate male authority (Hayes 1996:22). Any betrayal of male control is an insult to male honor; given the constant threat of betrayal, demonstrations of masculinity through a virile sexuality form an essential element in competitive displays between men (Gilmore 1996). The marked differentiation of the sexes justifies a double standard of morality. Men are given the freedom of car-nal love independent of reproduction, while for women, sexual relations are joined to the obligation to conceive, give birth, and raise children within marriage.

Unlike the northern version of modern Euro-American culture, in which biological sex is the basis of gender classification crosscut by the homosexual/heterosexual dichotomy, in Brazil, the core gender opposi-tion is based on sexuality, that is, the position taken in sexual inter-course. Brazilian gender ideology is based on the distinction between those who penetrate—the active (*atividade*), defined as masculine—and those who are penetrated—the passive (*passividade*), defined as femi-nine.

This ideology shapes the meanings of sexual relations between males and females and also between individuals of the same sex. The act of penetration of the female body by the male in sexual intercourse is the powerful act—in a concrete and metaphorical sense—that proclaims male superiority, linking male and female bodies in a relation of (male) dominance and (female) submission. Penetration symbolically expresses the hierarchical power relations at the heart of the patriarchal gender system. It is the central symbol of sexual relations and indeed, symbolically, all gender differences. Whether penetration actually occurs or is merely implied, it is key to the sex/gender system of Brazil.

The emphasis of the Brazilian sex/gender system is reflected—and reinforced—by the language with which Brazilians speak about the body and its practices and about sexuality and gender (Parker 1995:243). In common usage, position in sexual intercourse is expressed by the verbs "to eat" (*comer*) and "to give" (*dar*). Comer describes the male's active penetration and domination of the female and is used in different contexts as a synonym for the verbs "to possess" (*possuir*) or "to conquer" (*vencer*).

Dar is used to describe the female's passive submission to her male partner in her role of being penetrated during intercourse. Just as comer is used to describe various forms of domination through reference to the relations of gender, dar is also used to imply submission, subjugation, and passivity in varied contexts, from politics to sports, in which victors are said to have "eaten" their opponents. Thus, even the simplest verbal exchanges in Brazil reinforce the association of sexual atividade and passividade with relations of power and domination between men and women.

Through the act of eating, the active partner metaphorically consumes the passive, while through the act of giving, the passive partner offers herself/himself up to be possessed. The act of penetration thus also defines categories of persons: husbands are associated with those who "eat," wives with those who "give."

GENDER DIVERSITY:
TRAVESTÍS, BICHAS, AND VIADOS

This model of the relationship between males and females is central to Brazilian understandings of gender diversity, which focus on the effeminate passive male homosexual, who, depending on the region of Brazil and the social situation, is variously called bicha (literally bug, pest, or female animal), viado (literally, deer), or travestí (from the verb to cross-dress). Although these gender variants readily self-identify as homosexual, in the traditional sex/gender system, the term homosexual was not applied to the male-acting and penetrating partner in a same-sex sexual relationship. Thus, bichas, viados, and travesitís are "produced" through the application of the distinction between atividad and passividade to sexual relations between individuals of the same sex, not soley by virtue of their sexual orientation.

Because the most important criterion of the Brazilian sex/gender ideology is the sexual and social roles people play, not their sexual orientation, or even their biological sex (Fry 1986; Parker 1991), a male who enters into a sexual relationship with another male does not necessarily sacrifice his masculinity, so long as he performs the penetrating, active, masculine role during sexual intercourse and conducts himself as a male within society. The active male in same-sex sexual relations is an unmarked male—he falls into no special category of gender nonconformity. He does not regard himself as a homosexual and is not regarded as one by society. Same-sex sexual practices are reported as a common introduction to sexual activity for many Brazilian men during adolescence, and those in the active role are not stigmatized. Indeed, as part of the drive to dominate sexually, penetrating another male is sometimes claimed as an indication of a supervirile masculine identity (Parker 1995:245).

A male is a man (*homem* or *macho*) until he is accused of or proved to have given, in which case he becomes a bicha (or viado). If a male accepts that social role, he becomes a "real bicha." Taking on this role publicly is called *solta plumas*, literally "releases feathers" (from the importance of feathers in Carnaval, the annual pre-Lenten period of revelry, similar to the American Mardi Gras), which is particularly associated with bichas because of the Carnaval theme of inversion. A real bicha is assumed to be sexually a pasivo.

In Brazil, as in other "gender organized" systems of same-sex sexual relationships, the sexually receptive partner is expected to enact other aspects of the feminine gender role: to behave and/or sound and/or dress in ways appropriate to women. Once this role is imputed to an individual, it seriously damages his *masculinidade,* unalterably transforming and degrading him, as he becomes a symbolic female through his sexual role.

But bichas, viados, and travestís do not merely dress and act like women; they also transform their bodies (Kulick 1997; 1998). Boys who self-identify as travestís may begin ingesting or injecting female hormones as early as age 10 or 12, in order to develop breasts and give their bodies feminine contours. These hormones, which are either medications for combating estrogen deficiency in women or oral contraceptives, are cheap and available in Brazil. Travestís also use (most frequently industrial plastic) silicone for implants in order to create the fleshy thighs, expansive hips, and prominent buttocks that are the focus of the Brazilian ideal of feminine beauty (for a variety of aesthetic, practical, and medical reasons, silicone is not used for breast implants [Kulick 1997:576]).

In spite of their bodily modifications, however, travestís believe that a travestí is not a woman and can never be one, because "God created them male and their sex can never be changed" (Kulick 1998:193ff). This is a significant contrast to Western transsexuals and also to the hijras, whom travestís resemble in other ways. Unlike hijras, travestís do not want to get rid of their penises; they believe that sex-change operations do not produce women, but only castrated homosexuals. Furthermore, travestís believe that without a penis semen cannot leave the body and the trapped semen will eventually travel to the brain and cause madness. Thus, in a seeming paradox, simultaneously with their determined desire for a feminine body, travestís value their male genitals and "gasp in horror" at the thought of an amputation, which would mean the loss of an ability to have an erection or an orgasm (Kulick 1997:577). In yet another seeming paradox, travestís keep their penises hidden, that is, "imprisoned" between their legs, which is an important bodily practice in their daily public appearances, in their work as prostitutes, and in deference to their boyfriends' (*maridos*) masculine identities.

Unlike Western transsexuals, travestís modify their bodies not because they feel themselves to be women, but because they feel themselves to be "like women"—in their behavior, appearance, and particularly, in their relationships with men (Kulick 1997:577). A common—and crucial—theme in travestís' identities is that they experience themselves as travestís in connection with their sexual attraction to men, specifically in their desire for, and participation in, anal penetration. This attraction motivates their feminized bodily modifications and is central

Brazilian travestís often spend time in Europe working as prostitutes in order to earn more money than they can in Brazil. (Photograph by David Schrier.)

to their occupation as prostitutes and to their intimate relations with their maridos. Unlike modern Euro-American culture, travestí relations with men are not characterized as homosexual; rather they are viewed as "heterogenderal," because the relationship is culturally defined by the social/sexual differences in gender, not by the sameness of (male) bodies and sexual orientation.

Travestís' maridos (like some hijras' husbands) are typically attractive, muscular, tattooed young men with little education or income. They are not pimps, although they are supported by the travestí; rather, they move in with the travestí for "passion" and are kicked out on the same basis. Maridos regard themselves, and are regarded by their travestí girlfriends, as men. Since one of the defining characteristics of a "man" is that he will not be interested in another male's penis, the marido keeps his manhood by penetrating the travestí. Although some travestís express pleasure in taking the active sexual role, they also claim that this role would then cause them to lose respect for the marido, who would be transformed into a viado, or a "bicha incubada" (incubating bicha) in their eyes (Kulick 1998:96ff; Fry 1995:205). When a bicha or travestí learns that her man "gives" and has thus become a bicha, the humiliation is intense; no self-respecting bicha would admit to being penetrated by another bicha. The occasional "anything goes" sexual relationship in which no clear line is drawn between the male who "eats" and the male who "gives" is looked down upon. It is jokingly—and derogatorily—called lesbianism, referring to the bichas' view that lesbians don't really have (proper) sex (Fry 1995:204). Thus, within the bicha/travestí subculture, the norms of the heterosexual world are replicated; masculinity is associated with penetration and those who do not adhere to the active/passive distinction are stigmatized.

The verbalized commitment to this heterogender sexual norm sometimes contrasts, however, with actual behavior. On the streets travestís know they are valued for their possession of a penis; clients will often request to see or feel it before payment, and clients frequently request anal penetration. But even as travestís comply, they consider it an inversion of their normal practice and charge a higher price (Cornwall 1994:120).

MEN AND NOT-MEN: THE BRAZILIAN BINARY

Sex/gender diversity becomes meaningful only within each culture's distinctive sex/gender system. Thus, while travestís are not-men (or "failed men") they are not, like the hijra, considered an in-between or third gender, though they are sometimes described this way in the popular media. Nor are travestís considered as a kind of a woman, either by themselves or by others, although as prostitutes they are symbolically and socially "fallen" women and as such are doubly victimized.

Anthropologist Don Kulick (1997:579) explains travestís in terms of a Brazilian sex/gender system based on a dichotomy whose opposing categories are not men and women but rather men and not-men. The travestís are the example *par excellence* that the Brazilian sex/gender dichotomy is based on sexuality, rather than anatomy.

While biological differences are hardly ignored in Brazil, the definition of gender depends not merely on the possession of genitals, but on what they are used for. Travestís reiterate the Brazilian view that the locus of gender difference is the act of penetration. If one *only* penetrates, one is a man, but if one gets penetrated *one is not a man*; one is either a woman or a bicha/viado (Kulick 1997:580). The enjoyment of being penetrated classifies travestís with women: because they already share a gender with women (although they make no claims to be women), they do not need to change their sex. Losing their penises would add nothing and would be a loss of both pleasure and income.

Since travestís are classified with (not as) women, they are expected to share all the qualities of women, particularly the desire to attract and be attractive to persons of the opposite gender (men). An important part of this attraction—for women as for travestís—is as a subject for the male gaze: in Brazil, female bodies are extraordinarly looked at, and men do the looking. This emphasis on the importance of a bodily aesthetic in sexual relations and definitions of gender leads travestís to make extravagent attempts to incorporate Brazilian cultural ideals of beauty in their bodies, drawing them not to resistance, but to reinforcement, of the dominant patriarchal and hierarchical sex/gender system of which they are a part.

ATTITUDES TOWARD GENDER DIVERSITY

Attitudes toward gender diversity in Brazil are best described as complex, sometimes contradictory, and ambivalent. On the one hand, gender diversity is central to Carnaval, itself a positive icon of Brazilian culture both to Brazilians themselves and to the outside world. In Carnaval cross-dressing and gender inversion are prominent, not only for travestís, but also for gender-conforming men. Travestís often appear in Brazilian television soap operas, and Brazilians' open attitudes toward sexuality are reflected in the apparently universal willingness of men in Brazil to publicly admire the travestí, Roberta Close (who subsequently became a transsexual), as the most beautiful woman in Brazil (Kottack 1990:31).

At the same time that some travestís may be cultural icons, however, most travestís are actually treated very badly. In upsetting the culturally prescribed fit between biological sex and social gender, bichas, viados, and travestís are perceived as failed men, not as women. Thus they are viewed and severely stigmatized as a failure on both social and biological counts: unable to realize their biological potential as men because of inappropriate sexual behavior, they are equally unable to cross the boundaries of gender due to their inability to reproduce.

Travestís and bichas tend to be ostracized in mainstream society and find employment only in highly marginal lines of work or in jobs traditionally reserved for women. In some parts of Brazil they are called *marginais*, a term whose meaning of "marginal" is much stronger than its English translation. They are associated not only with sexually deviant behavior but with criminality and have been noted by several anthropologists as being among the most marginalized, feared, and despised groups in Brazil (Cornwall 1994; Kulick 1996:4; 1998). Travestís are regularly victims of police brutality and even murder, and until recently, many would not come out of doors during the day and were confined to the worst areas of cities. Most come from very poor backgrounds, and many have severe health and drug abuse problems. Travestís do engage in criminal acts, mainly their well-known practice of robbing their customers, and their association with homosexuality, prostitution, and now AIDS increases the stigma and censure they experience. In the streets often they are addressed mockingly as "Mister," a contemptuous way of refusing to acknowledge their gender.

The harshest scorn is reserved for unattractive travestís. Anthropologist Don Kulick (1998) suggests that perhaps the harassment on the street, which takes the form of verbally mocking travestís' gender as "not-men," is less a reaction to them as gender-crossers than a reaction against unattractiveness in people (women and other not-men) whose job it is to make themselves attractive to men. Travestís like Roberta Close and others who meet or even exceed Brazilian ideals of feminine beauty are not mocked, and ordinary men even seem willing to acknowledge them as legitimate sexual objects (Kottack 1990). Thus, in yet another permutation in the Brazilian sex/gender system, some of the hostility against travestís may be a reaction against them as failed women, not failed men.

AFRO-BRAZILIAN RELIGION

Gender diversity in Brazil is associated with Afro-Brazilian religions. While pasivos are generally stigmatized in Latin America, women and pasivos dominate the leadership in Afro-Brazilian religions. These religions, focused on possession trance and oriented toward providing spiritual help and protection for their followers, are found predominantly in the north and northeast regions of Brazil, areas that contain a majority of African-Brazilians and the poor, and where gender relationships are generally more rigid than in the industrialized, more highly educated, and more socially mobile urbanized south.

The most familiar Afro-Brazilian religions are called *Candomble* (or Macumba) (see Fry 1995; Wafer 1991). Their main spirits are *orixas* of West African, primarily Yoruba, origin, who are also identified with saints of the Roman Catholic Church. This syncretism developed during the colonial period in Brazil, when the slaves concealed their African gods behind the masks of Christian saints. Under the leadership of the major orixas are a host of lesser spirits essential to day-to-day ritual activity. Candomble is organized into houses called *terreiros,* which are hierarchically structured around a female or male leader called mother or father of the saint. Each terreiro is autonomous and competes against other terreiros for followers, clients, and resources.

Candomble practitioners or followers are called sons- or daughters-of-saints and owe their allegiance to the particular mother- or father-of-saint of their chosen terreiro. Thus the terreiro operates as a hierarchically organized extended family with allegiance and obligation being the duty of the followers and guidance and spiritual care the responsibility of the leader. Within the terreiro women as well as men may assume the role of patriarchal family head, and the father- or mother-of-saints maintains control over the followers. The modeling of the terreiro on the kin-

Women and male gender variants occupy important roles in Yoruba possession religions, which spread to the New World. (Photograph by Serena Nanda.)

ship structure of a family proscribes sexual relations among the followers and between the followers and the terreiro leaders.

Candomble religious life is expressed in public dances and festivals,
ritual offerings, divinatory sessions, and initiation rituals, all of which
involve the participation of diverse spirits. Various rituals and services
are also provided for nonpracticing believers, who approach the religion
as clients in search of spiritual assistance. The most significant ritual
event is initiation, which centers around possession trance. Once initiated, a follower is obligated to his/her possessing spirits and patron deities who are called upon to guarantee good fortune, health, success, and
survival. The member's obligation to the orixas requires regular offerings, but most importantly, the follower must "receive" (*receber*) the
orixas in regular ritual seances, which take the form of possession
trances (Hayes 1996:15).

Possession trance or "receiving the spirits" establishes contact
between the human realm and the divine and transforms initiates into
followers of the saints, distinguishing them from clients and spectators.
Other, noninitiated tereirro members act as ritual assistants, drummers,
or perform the animal sacrifices that are a source of the sacrificial blood
necessary to nourish the gods. Spirits ritually inhabit the body of a follower in possession trance, as well as inhabiting their special "altar," a
collection of symbolic representations of the spirit that contain the
spirit's power. The medium dances while possessed and also speaks with
clients, giving advice and ritual protection. Theatricality is an important
aspect of the performance, and terreiros are elaborately decorated with
statues of spirits, paper flags and streamers, flashing lights, and so forth.
Mediums are expected to dress well, and terreiro members pride themselves in their singing and dancing skills. The ritual ends with the depar-
ture of the spirits, although mediums may remain possessed for hours or
even days afterward (Hayes 1996).

LINKS BETWEEN CANDOMBLE
AND GENDER DIVERSITY

Early descriptions of Afro-Brazilian religions noted the predominance of women as religious leaders, emphasizing the warm and nurtur-
ing qualities of women as central to the spiritual services that the cults
offered (Landes 1946). After the 1940s, however, Candomble leaders were
increasingly effeminate pasivos. Although some observers criticized this
shift as a corruption of traditional Yoruba "matriarchy," Candomble's
association with gender diversity appears to be consistent with the sexual ambiguity that characterizes Yoruba religion in its homeland (Matory
1996). Among the Yoruba, transvestism, feminine gestures, and feminine

occupations are marked among male possession priests (Matory 1994:170ff). During and soon after initiation, Yoruba possession priests are called brides of the god and don women's clothing during initiation. Both male and female priests wear feminine hairstyles and feminine cosmetics and jewelry.

The view that the pasivo presence in Candomble continues rather than disrupts Yoruba tradition complements earlier functionalist explanations of the association between pasivos and Afro-Brazilian possession religions. Several of these explanations focus on marginality. Although even upper-class Brazilians seek the magical services of Candomble, Afro-Brazilian religions are considered deviant in the dominant Brazilian culture (in the past, these religions were outlawed by the Brazilian government; this has changed as the government now views the Afro-Brazilian religions as an important tourist attraction). The negative association of Candomble with the poor and the "superstitiousness" of African religions, as well as with haunts of immorality and crime, make them socially and spatially marginal in Brazilian society. Terreiros, for example, are most often located on the outskirts of cities and are difficult to find.

Thus, one widespread explanation for the association of Candomble with pasivos, and indeed, more widely with "deviant" sexuality as well as with women, suggests the cults provide a cultural space where women and pasivos, stigmatized and oppressed in the larger society, can exercise spiritual powers from which they receive otherwise unavailable financial and social rewards (Fry 1986). Another functional explanation for the association of gender nonconformists with Afro-Brazilian religions is that in the terreiro and its activities, pasivos may give rein to their "femininity" through association with the predominantly female membership of the religions and through possession by female spirits (Fry 1986). Additionally, once the religious leadership becomes associated in the popular imagination with pasivos for whatever reasons, other men will not want to risk their masculinity by being associated with them (Fry 1995:201).

Anthropologist Peter Fry also suggests that since both pasivos and possession trance religions are defined as deviant in relation to dominant Brazilian values, marginal individuals would find a congenial role in them. More particularly, he notes, the very deviance of the pasivos enhances their ability to be religious leaders: to be defined by society as defiling and dangerous may be an advantage to those in a role in which they exercise magical power. In this sense, Fry views pasivos as having an advantage over both women and men as Candomble leaders (Fry 1995:195). The enhanced magical power of pasivos comes from being associated with the potential destructiveness, yet also with the power of "disorder" that occurs in the meeting of the secular and the divine. As with hijras and American Indian gender variants, the relation of magical power to the margins of society is easily associated with those defined as sexually ambiguous.

Other explanations of pasivo success in Candomble emphasize that it is the *combination* of the masculine and the feminine that gives them an advantage (Fry 1995:207). J. Lorand Matory notes that in Afro-Brazilian religions, despite the important presence of women priestesses, the gender of the divine agency defining the priestess's authority is often male. Pasivos enjoy some of the unique ritual prerogatives of men in Candomble and also are not subject to the prohibitions placed on the participation of menstruating women (Matory 1996:23). While both men and women must cleanse themselves from the pollution of sexual relations before and during ritual activity, pasivos are subject only to the lesser defilement of males and are more easily cleansed than women. Yet, at the same time, pasivos, as women, are exempt from the taboos on males engaging in cooking and embroidery, both of which are important to the success of the terreiro. In addition, pasivos do not have the obligations of marriage and kinship and can thus devote all their earnings to the terreiro, increasing its material display and thus enhancing confidence in its efficacy and winning larger numbers of committed followers. Pasivos are also considered more artistic than either men or women and are therefore perceived as better equipped to organize and participate in ritual. Pasivos thus are not merely a "pale imitation of a woman," but rather combine certain key aspects of the "normal" male and female roles, which they can manipulate to their own advantage.

PENETRATION, POSSESSION TRANCE, AND GENDER DIVERSITY IN CANDOMBLE

Symbolic explanations for pasivo predominance in Candomble are also relevant. The meanings of penetration and possession in Candomble both reinforce and resist the dominant norms of gendered relationships in Brazil and help explain the association of Candomble with women and pasivos (Hayes 1996). In Candomble the relationship between the spirits and humans—between the gods and the followers who incorporate them—is analogically associated with that of male-to-females through the metaphor of penetration. Thus the term describing possession is *dar santo* ("to give saint"): the role of the human being (whether man or woman) possessed by the spirit in trance is identified with the female who gives herself over to sexual pentration by the male. The Candomble priests who are possessed are called "horses" or "mounts" of the gods, who "ride" them, again recalling the submissive or passive role of women in sexual relations. During possession, the god "mounts" the priest, as a rider does a horse or as a male does his female sexual partner. The role of metaphorical male in this relation between humans and spirits is occupied by the spirits, who *penetrate*, who ride their mounts (*cavalos*: horses) in order to express their desires, chastise their followers, advise, or merely to "play." This makes sense of the fact that women—and pasivos—are more appropriate for the role of *filho-de-santos* ("followers-of-the-saints") than men.

For if women, who receive the gods in trance, thus mimic the normative male-female relations in which penetration (spiritual or sexual) defines them as female, it follows that men who are ridden by the gods are deemed pasivo, for they assume the female role of being penetrated as opposed to the normative male role of penetration. Thus, spiritual penetration by the (male) gods for a male is equivalent to becoming a pasivo: it involves a renunciation of masculine atividade in favor of the most passive role, that of *dando santo* ("giving saint"). As anthropologist Jim Wafer describes it (1991:18), humans are "female" in relation to all the spirits when they go into trance. Humans "give" offerings so that the spirits may "eat."

In the religious context of possession trance, then, normative gender relationships are reiterated and reinforced. But even as trance reiterates normative gender classifications, it reinterprets and reevaluates them (Hayes 1996). Within the religious context, being penetrated is empowering rather than subordinating, and it is prestigious rather than degraded (if only because of the high status of the gods in relation to humans). This helps explain the attraction of women and pasivos to the Afro-Brazilian possession religions. In this respect, possession trance is similar to other religious situations (such as the power of the hijras), which have long been associated with alternative interpretations and revaluations of social reality, creating situations in which normative systems of classification may be questioned, transgressed, manipulated, or reversed and in which those who are marginal in the real world become central in religious ritual (see Turner 1969).

CHANGING SEX/GENDER IDEOLOGIES

In Brazil, as increasingly in many contemporary cultures, several sex/gender ideologies coexist. Along with the traditional emphasis on sexual practice as determinative of gender identity, a modern Euro-American "medical" model of sex/gender relations entered Brazil in the late-nineteenth and early-twentieth centuries. This model emphasized same-sex sexual relations as detrimental to the health of society (Parker 1999). This model continues to be relevant but in the last three decades

has been challenged by a (postmodern) gay ideology, in which both partners in a same-sex sexual relationship are viewed equally in terms of
their sexual orientation. This model, which continues the homosexual/
heterosexual divide of the medical model, but without its pejorative con-
notions, is gaining a foothold in the more highly industrialized urban
centers of the south (Rio and Sao Paulo) as well as among the more
wealthy and educated classes throughout Brazil. The traditional pattern
continues to dominate in the north and northeast among the rural, less
educated and poorer classes. Brazil, then, like Thailand and the Philippines, described in chapter 5, is most accurately characterized as having
not one, but several sex/gender ideologies, related to each other in complex and sometimes contradictory ways.

Chapter Four

Liminal Gender Roles
in Polynesia

In this chapter we encounter sex/gender diversity in Polynesia, the "many islands" of the Pacific. The Pacific islands are commonly divided into Melanesia and Polynesia. Although individuals of "in-between" sex/ gender are acknowledged and linguistically marked in Melanesia (see Herdt 1996b), sex/gender diversity is not as culturally elaborated there as it is in Polynesia. In Melanesian cultures, male homosexuality is an age-defined, often mandatory, and transitory role, frequently associated with elaborate male initiation and part of a cult of masculinity in which ingesting semen was considered essential for the growth of boys into men (Herdt 1981). It is not associated with sex/gender diversity. In Polynesia, on the other hand, in spite of significant cultural variation, there are also some important shared cultural patterns that provide a common context for long-standing and deep-rooted traditions of gender diversity.

The local economies of Polynesia primarily depend on horticulture and exploiting products of the sea, though a cash economy is now also important almost everywhere. The more complex Polynesian societies are characterized by social ranking systems consisting of chiefs, nobles, and commoners. Rank is determined by position—birth order and gene-alogical closeness to the chief—and kinship is thus an essential source of political, economic, and social power. Competition for power and prestige is a central cultural preoccupation for men, although women, too, have informal avenues of influence. Traditionally, elaborate systems of taboos restricted interaction between different social categories, including men and women, and these rules influence behavior even today.

Gender relations in Polynesia are complementary, with men and women having their own spheres of work, sociality, and behavioral norms, though the intensity of gender role differentiation varies among the islands. Two important widespread gender norms in Polynesia are respect relationships between brothers and sisters (or those classified as such, i.e., males and females of the same generation) and the division of women's roles into the more positively valued virginal "girl," and the less valued, mature wife, who has had at least one child (Mageo 1992; Shore 1981).

Although Polynesia has, since its discovery by Europeans, figured in the Western imagination as a place of unrestricted and casual sexuality, including a "tolerance" of gender diversity, Polynesian expression of sexuality is, as in all societies, culturally shaped and constrained. Sexual expression, gender relations, and attitudes toward gender diversity are all grounded in the Polynesian cultural emphasis (also important in Thailand) on the contrast between socially controlled and uncontrolled aspects of human existence. "Good" behavior is that which conforms to social roles and is characterized by respect and restraint of personal impulses. "Bad," "disgusting," and "selfish" behavior is that motivated by personal desire, impulsiveness, and self-gratification (Shore 1981:195). Sexuality, in particular, is associated with personal desire. The values of social role and emotional and behavioral restraint are exemplified in many aspects of Polynesian sexuality and gender relations: the idealization of virginity; a distinction between women as wives and women as sisters; and the importance of kinship relations, particularly those between brother and sister, as the basis for appropriate, and restrained, social and sexual interaction. Gender diversity in Polynesia needs to be understood within the context of these (and other) cultural patterns, which are discussed below.

GENDER LIMINAL MALE ROLES

The main cultural feature of gender diversity in Polynesia involves males who appropriate certain feminine characteristics. The practice of some male individuals adopting attributes associated with women is traditional and deeply embedded in much of Polynesia. These gender variant roles have different names in different places, reflecting Polynesian cultural variation (Besnier 1996). In Tahiti and contemporary Hawaii, the role is called *māhū*. (Although there is little historical documentation of female māhūs in Tahiti, these roles may also be available to women [Elliston 1999]). In Samoa, male gender variants are called *fa'afafine*, which literally means "like a woman"; in Tonga, the term is *fakaleitī*, whose root, *leitī*, is borrowed from the English word "lady"; and in Tuva in the Gilbertese islands, the term is *pinapinaaine*.

In spite of the time-depth of gender diversity in Polynesia, it appears to be less institutionalized than in some other cultures—thus it

Hermaphrodite fig-
ures, combining
male and female
anatomy, play an
important role in
creation stories all
over the Pacific
islands. (Photograph
by Ravinder Nanda.)

can be termed liminal. Unlike India, native North America, and Brazil,
for example, in Polynesia there is no consistently articulated ideology
associated with gender variants, no uniformly consistent role with which
they are identified, and the boundaries of the role are "porous": a man
can move into the role and then move out of it in later life. In Polynesian
social life, behavior and identity are generally a matter of appropriate
situational context, and this is also true for the enactment of gender
diversity. Thus, there is substantial variability among gender variant
individuals, and also within an individual's behavior in different situations and over a lifetime (Besnier 1996). At the same time, in some
places, for example Tahiti, social acceptance of gender variant roles is
significantly legitimated by an individual's long-term participation in
these roles, frequently manifested since childhood (Elliston 1999:236).

Because of cultural and individual variation, defining Polynesian gender diversity is problematic. Although māhū is translated in Tahiti as "half-man, half-woman," the māhū is not a well-defined third gender like the hijras in India or the gender variants among American Indians. Elliston (1999:236) defines the māhū in Tahiti "as a gender category for persons who deploy and participate in complex combinations of masculine and feminine gender signs and practices," with the dominant gender role being that opposite to the individual's anatomy.

Regarding male gender diversity in Polynesia generally, the most important of these "gender signs and practices" appears to be engaging in women's work. Other important feminine gender markers adopted by males are feminine dress, speech tones and nonverbal gestures, and dance styles. Also noteworthy is the association of gender-nonconforming males with girls and young women in friendship groups, which, given the importance of sex-segregated social gatherings in Polynesia, is significant.

Mature men have the most important ritual roles throughout the Pacific Islands, roles from which male gender liminals are excluded. (Photograph by Raymond Kennedy.)

Although sexuality (sexual orientation or sexual practices) does not define Polynesian gender diversity, gender variant sexuality is assumed to be consistent with the adopted gender, with males taking male sexual partners and females taking female lovers. Gender variant males are associated with certain sexual practices, and these play an important part in their personal identities and economic strategies, as well as being an important factor in social attitudes towards them.

In contrast to India, native North America, and to a lesser extent, Brazil, Polynesian gender diversity is not associated with religion nor does it have sacred meanings. It is, however, associated with "rituals of reversal," that is, secular cultural performances that involve spontaneous, clowning, and uninhibited behavior that is normally disparaged and repressed. Gender diversity therefore is functionally integrated into some Polynesian societies.

Given the high variability in gender variant roles, the marginality of gender variant persons in Polynesian societies, their association with "rituals of reversal," and the limited contexts in which gender diversity is enacted, ethnographer Niko Besnier suggests that the term "gender liminal" is more accurate than third gender. In addition to not being highly institutionalized, gender variants in Polynesia mainly derive their meanings from the normative Polynesian binary gender system of man and woman, rather than any distinctive features or an independent status of their own. As in Brazil (but in contrast to the Western transsexual), the Polynesian gender liminal individual crosses genders in acting "like a woman" but is not viewed as having become a woman. He is, then, suspended between man and woman, being neither, and at the same time having elements of both.

Since kinship in Polynesia is structured on the basis of a fundamental opposition and hierarchical complementarity between male and female roles, there is no room for an autonomous, institutionalized in-between gender. What best seems to fit the Polynesian situation, according to Besnier, is that gender liminal individuals are men who *borrow* certain social and cultural attributes and symbols normatively associated with women. These attributes may differ in kind and number and may be foregrounded or backgrounded in different contexts, even occasionally shed if needed. This borrowing is the process that gives rise to a loosely defined, gender liminal identity.

HISTORICAL CONTEXTS

The degree to which contemporary gender liminality is the same as that in precontact Polynesia is uncertain. While the earliest Europeans in Polynesia in the late-eighteenth century commented on gender diversity, missionaries in the nineteenth and early-twentieth centuries by and large did not. European colonial regimes differed in Polynesia but in most cases attempted to suppress what gender diversity they found. Anthropologists in the early-twentieth century hardly mentioned the subject. As with other aspects of Polynesian sexuality, the social "acceptance" of gender diversity tended to be romanticized in some anthropological accounts in the mid-1950s, as well as in later accounts by gay observers. Only in the 1970s did some relatively detailed ethnography on Polynesian gender diversity begin to make its appearance. Thus, one of the unanswered questions in Polynesia is the extent to which contemporary gender liminality represents a continuity with gender liminality in the past, or a break and new cultural construction.

As in native North America, when Europeans first encountered Polynesia, they immediately noticed the presence of gender diversity and associated it with their own notions of homosexual sodomy. An eighteenth-century account suggests some of the features of this role in Tahiti (note the comparison the writer makes with the eunuchs—possibly he means hijras here—of India, who were already well known and much commented on by European travelers):

> "[The māhū] are like the Eunichs [sic] in India but they are not castrated. They never cohabit with women but live as they do. They pick their beards out and dress as women, dance and sing with them and are as effeminate in their voice. They do women's employment and excell [sic] in some crafts. It is said that they converse with men as familiar as women do." (Morrison, in Levy 1973:130)

Captain Bligh, commander of the *Bounty*, infamous because of the mutiny of its crew, also noted the behavior of the māhū, observing that they participated in the same ceremonies as women and ate as women did. The māhū's effeminate speech led Bligh to believe they were castrated, but he later found out that they were not, noting, however, that "things equally disgusting were committed" (referring to their sexual relations with men). Bligh was told that the māhū were selected when they were boys and kept with the women solely for "the caresses of the men." When, in order to learn more about them, Bligh had one māhū remove his loin cloth, he noted that

> "He had the appearance of a woman, his yard [penis] and testicles being so drawn in under him, having the art from custom of keeping them in this position . . . [His genitals] are very small and the testicles remarkably so, being not larger than a boy's five or six years old, and very soft as in a state of decay or a total incapacity of being larger, so that . . . he appeared . . . a Eunuch [as much as if] his stones were away. The women treat him as one of their sex and he observed every restriction that they do, and is equally respected and esteemed." (Bligh, in Levy 1973:130–31)

Bligh goes on to report that the men who had sexual relations with a māhū "have their beastly pleasures gratified between his thighs" but they denied practicing sodomy. A nineteenth-century account declared that the māhū fellated the man he had relations with, swallowing the semen, which was believed to give them strength (Levy 1973:135). Contemporary accounts note similar behavior, and some Tahitian men talk of the exceptional strength of the māhū.

APPROPRIATIONS OF THE FEMININE

The defining criterion for the māhū is that he *publicly* engages in the occupations and activities of women. Speaking of the māhū in one Tahitian rural district, ethnographer Robert Levy says: "His feminine role taking is demonstrated for the villagers because he performs women's household activities, cleans the house, takes care of babies, braids coconut palm leaves into thatching plaits" (1973:140). The māhū in another district associates with the adolescent girls of the village and walks with his arm interlocked with theirs, "a behavior otherwise seen only among people of the same sex."

In Polynesia women and men are associated with different economic roles. In Samoa, for example, males do the "heavy" and instrumental work of directly providing food, whether from gardening or from the sea, while women are linked with "light" work that is largely decorative and associated with the household and the village, such as keeping the village clean and weaving the fine mats that are used in Polynesian rituals of exchange (Mead 1971; Shore 1981:203). Gender nonconforming males do the light work of women and, as among American Indians, are thought to excel in women's occupations. In urban areas of Polynesia, gender nonconformists are considered excellent secretaries and are coveted domestic help (Besnier 1997).

Polynesian gender distinctions of dress may seem small to Westerners but are important gender markers. In Samoa, for example, gendered dress styles are well defined, particularly in the way the *lavalava* (sarong) is tied (Shore 1981:206). Although men and women may use the same material and colors, men leave a large end of their lavalava flopping in the front. Women, in contrast, do not let the end hang out, but rather tuck the ends inside the waist. This difference is remarked upon; a man can convey a gender transformation by consistently tying his lavalava in a feminine style. Although gender variants are often referred to as "transvestites" in the anthropological accounts of Polynesia, they generally do not cross-dress on a permanent basis, though transvestism does provide a vehicle of self-identification and social presentation for gender variant males (and females). In Tahiti, Elliston reports (1999:236) that most male māhūs wear a *pareu*, a garment worn mainly by women, but in other parts of Polynesia much of the gender variant males' transvestism occurs within the context of stage performances.

The speech differences associated with men and women in Polynesian societies also provide a vehicle for gender variation. Male gender variants adopt women's speech patterns and their "high pitched" tone of voice. Like women, male gender variants are also more "coquettishly" concerned with their physical appearance and often wear flowers, garlands, perfume, and heavy makeup—accessories generally associated with young women. Other "feminine" characteristics include a feminine manner of walking and feminine gestures.

Perhaps because of the emphasis on role playing as a central and valued part of Polynesian life, gender variance also has aspects of a role that is being played and, indeed, is largely played on stage. This aspect of Polynesian culture underlines the view that gender variant statuses there are not necessarily permanent. For example, although Tahitians generally claim that changing one's sex is not possible, it is possible to stop being a māhū, "as one can discontinue being a chief." Anthropologist Robert Levy noted that in the village he studied, one man in his early adolescence had dressed from time to time in girls' clothes and was thus considered a māhū but in his early twenties "cast off" the role. It was assumed in the village that this was the end of it and that the person was now leading an ordinary masculine life (Levy, 1973:133). At the same time, the māhū is generally described as "natural" and thought to "have been born that way," in contrast to "homosexuals" who are believed to choose their roles when they are adults.

SEXUALITY AND GENDER LIMINALITY

Although it was the sexual behavior of the māhū in Tahiti that drew immediate and disapproving attention from Europeans, it is clear from both historical and contemporary accounts that the māhū role involved, and involves today, more than same-sex sexual practices (Besnier 1996; Elliston 1999; Shore 1981). Same-sex sexual relations alone do not define the liminal gender category in Polynesia; as Deborah Elliston (1999:236) notes, the māhū is consistently associated with gender and his sexuality is consistently put in the background. As is true in many cultures, men who have sexual relations with the māhū are not considered in any way to be gender variants themselves. Nevertheless, Polynesian gender diversity *is* associated with a particular sexuality, however backgrounded. The māhū, fakaleitī, or pinapinaaine is the fellator and, as such, is seen as a substitute for a woman. While no stigma or shame is attached to their sexual partners, there is a potentially negative connotation that a person who seeks the māhū or his equivalent for a sexual partner does so because he could not obtain a woman.

All ethnographers confirm that Polynesian liminal genders are not the same as Western homosexuals. In contemporary Tahiti, homosexuality, called *raerae*, is considered a foreign (French) import and is differentiated from sexual relations with a māhū. Raerae refers to a person "who does not perform a female's village role and who dresses and acts like a man, but who indulges in exclusive or preferred sexual behavior with other men." Though there is some confusion over terms and categories, raerae seems to mean "sex-role reversal" and/or "sodomy"; it is also applied to a reversed role in sexual relations between a man and a woman (Levy 1973:140). While effeminate men may be described as māhūish, such an individual is assumed to be an ordinary man, involved in standard male activity, and engaged in normal heterosexual practices. In Samoa, there is no word for homosexual, and in any case, same-sex sexual play is viewed as part of a normal growing-up process for most boys (Mead 1971; Shore 1981).

The gender liminal role in Polynesia is not in any way imposed on men perceived as effeminate (in Polynesian terms), and it is unclear whether a physical anomaly is involved in recruitment to these roles. In Tahiti, one of Levy's māhū informants said that the māhū are not supercised (a traditional coming-of-age ceremony for boys that involves incisions made on the shaft of the penis) because a māhū's penis is too small, an observation made in the early contact period. On the other hand, based on one observation, Levy expressed the view that diminuitive genital size is not necessarily a physical correlate for the māhū role and that a boy might be "coached" into the role by his elders, perhaps just for their amusement, by dressing him in girls' clothes. If a male child seems determined to wear girls' clothes, adults will not stand in his way, and a child's insistence in some cases is felt to be "irresistible" (Levy, 1973:140).

In Samoa, also, gender nonconformity might well begin in childhood, and a family with few girls may even bring up a boy child as a girl, though most gender variant boys adopt transvestism voluntarily (Mageo 1992:450). Contrary to the benign image presented by Levy for Tahiti, in Samoa a boy's male relatives may beat him for wearing girls' clothes, though potential fa'afafine may receive support from their mothers who, as supervisors of the household, are more likely than men to notice—and condone—the young boy's preference for women's domestic chores.

In traditional Polynesia, a preference for same-sex sexual intimacy was not considered either a necessary or sufficient criterion for gender liminal status. Intimate and erotic same-sex sexual behavior by itself does not "brand" one as a gender variant. In fact it is expected to, and frequently does, occur in other contexts such as boarding schools or prisons, and sexual experimentation among teenaged boys appears to be a normal part of Polynesian development. Gender liminal adult males are not presupposed to have a history of or an identifiable preference for same-sex sexual relationships; indeed, the "assignment" of gender liminal status frequently takes place in childhood, before the awakening of sexual desires. Rather, in common with North American Indian gender variants, in Polynesia, sexual relations with men seems to be a possible *consequence* of a nonconforming male gender status, rather than its cause, prerequisite, or primary attribute (Besnier 1996; Elliston 1999).

There is little evidence on actual sexual behavior associated with gender liminality in Polynesia. Levy noted that māhūs perform fellatio on non-māhūs, who view the māhū as a convenient, pleasurable, relatively pressure-free alternative to women for the release of sexual tension. In Tonga and Tuvalu, Besnier reports that young men brag in private about anally penetrating the gender divergent male and engaging in sex between his thighs; although Besnier notes that māhūs take the "female" role in sexual relations "as recipient rather than inserter" (1997:9), he reports elsewhere that male gender nonconformists do sometimes act as inserters. A Polynesian male (as in India and Brazil) who takes the inserter position with another male is not linguistically distinguished or socially marginalized; because this practice is somewhat stigmatized as conveying an inability to find a woman, however, it is mainly associated with younger men. Married men are assumed to have sex only with women. And, similar to India, Brazil, Thailand and the Philippines, but in contrast to the West, gender nonconformists do not have sex with each other.

SEXUALITY AND SOCIAL STATUS

In spite of the "respect" that early Europeans attributed to gender liminal roles in traditional Polynesian societies, and in spite of their acceptance as "natural," today these roles do carry some social stigma, and the terms that define them can be, and often are, used derogatorily. This stigma, as well as the harassment and even the violence sometimes directed at gender variant individuals in some Polynesian societies, for example Tonga, is closely associated with their sexuality (Besnier 1997). Although sexuality cannot be viewed as the cause of male gender variance, it is today central to its contemporary definition, as perhaps it was in the past.

Gender liminals are almost always perceived as possible subjects of sexual conquest by men in Polynesia, although paradoxically, in Tonga, for example, fakaleitī are also seen as sexual predators (though some ethnographic observation suggests otherwise). In addition, while men must repay sexual favors from women with material goods, it is the fakaleitī who must spend money on his boyfriends for liquor, entertainment, and high-prestige consumer items (Besnier 1997:16). In Samoa and Tahiti the fa'afafine or the māhū may tease men in the same flirtatious way that women do, but even when not initiating a flirtation, they frequently will be the target of harassment and even physical violence, particularly from men in various states of inebriation (Besnier 1997). Gender liminal males are viewed as potential sexual "fair game" in a broader sense than women, who are to some extent protected by the classificatory brother-sister relationships so important in Polynesian social structure. This is particularly true for low-ranking gender liminal males; in Polynesian cultures, where social ranking is central to social structure, higher-ranking gender liminal males are somewhat protected by their social position.

The derogation of the gender liminal male is related to his feminine role in sexual relations. While sexual position (inserter or insertee) is not reported as a critical marker of female inferiority in Polynesia, as it is in Brazil, outside of special circumstances, such as in prison, a gender-conforming male would not take an insertee role, because it would mean that he would be subordinating himself to another, which "no man in his right mind would consent to." Male gender liminality is stigmatized on another basis in Polynesia: it is viewed as inherently promiscuous, transient, and lacking in significance. As Besnier so poignantly notes, "the gender liminal sexual partner, like the woman of loose virtue, is considered an eminently discardable and exploitable object" (1996:303). In Fiji, the gender liminal male as a sexual partner is analogized to a local, one-stringed musical instrument, whose tune is easily manipulated.

Besnier develops this theme by noting that in Polynesia, gender liminals' experience of sexuality, unlike that of women, is socially defined as falling outside the erotic. One expression of this is that they are consistently represented by others as "lacking the sexual anatomy of a normal adult man," with genitals "too small for circumcision," though this has not been demonstrated and does not appear to be true. Besnier views this inaccurate perception as a way of excluding gender liminals from adult erotic possibilities. They are, like children, held to be incapable of experiencing sexual desire, and the popular, though inaccurate, view is that the "sole purpose of the encounter" for gender liminal males is to satisfy the sexual needs of their partners.

Gender liminal male sexuality in Polynesia, then, contains some contradictions: gender liminals are significantly defined by their sexuality yet also traditionally are known by their feminine occupations; they are considered as both falling outside the range of normal adult male eroticism yet also are considered sexual predators; and they are like women in their sexual practices but are unlike women in that they pay for sexual favors. These contradictions are explained partly by Polynesian cultural variability, partly by the Polynesian concept of the person (discussed later), and partly, as in several other cultures discussed in this book, by the ambivalence of social attitudes toward them.

PERFORMING GENDER DIVERSITY

Gender liminal roles in Polynesia are particularly closely associated with secular performances and entertainment, the forms and functions of which are rooted in the culture, social structure, and gender relations of these societies. This seems true for both traditional performances, where male gender diversity is associated with spontaneous clowning and comic exaggerations, and contemporary contexts, where it is associated with cultural performances for tourists, beauty contests (to be further discussed for the Philippines), nightclub floor shows, and all-female gatherings, such as bridal showers (Mageo 1992).

There is a close association in Polynesia between performance, gender liminality, and reversals of the social order (reminiscent of the role hijras play in marriages where their performances expose the structural oppositions and conflicts between the bride's family and the groom's fam-

In many places in Polynesia, dancing is an opportunity for clowning behavior, which alludes to points of tension in social structure. Here, Fijian women perform this role, which is often also performed by gender variants. (Photo by Andrew Arno. Reprinted with the permission of Ablex Publishing Corporation © 1993. All rights reserved.)

ily). Performances in Polynesia, particularly dancing, have a strong anti-structural component. Different elements in the dances mirror some of the oppositional elements and tensions in society, including those between male and female, and between females as virginal "girls" and as mature, sexually active, wives and mothers (Mageo 1992; Shore 1981).

As noted, Polynesian cultures are characterized by an emphasis on decorum, emotional restraint, and respect behavior, especially where brothers and sisters are present. These norms particularly apply to discussing or expressing sexual matters in gender-mixed company. Gender liminality in Polynesia is associated, in contrast, with a lack of restraint and decorum, particularly regarding sexuality, and this makes gender liminal individuals particularly suitable for secular entertainments. Indeed, the sexually suggestive performances of, for example, the fa'afafine in contemporary Samoa suggest one explanation of their role: where the virgin girl is still the cultural ideal, the "outrageous" behavior of the fa'afafine provides a negative role model of how girls should not behave. In traditional Samoa, these antistructural performances were in fact performed by girls in the particular context of visiting villages other than their own, where the males would not fall into the categories of brothers. With the advent of Christianity, which is now thoroughly embedded as a source of Polynesian morality, these traditional elements of culture for the most part have been suppressed, and the norm-breaking nature of dance performances has to a large extent been taken over by the fa'afafine (Mageo 1992).

If the gender liminal person has a significant cultural function in contemporary Polynesia, as indicated above, the entertainments in which he performs are also functional from his own, subjective perspective: they are particularly appropriate venues for the expression and display of his femininity through parodic behavior; transvestism; feminine accessorizing, such as wearing makeup, flowers, and perfume; creativity in composing songs; and dancing (Besnier 1996:297). In addition, cultural performances provide an important avenue of prestige and economic reward for gender liminal males, who are seriously marginalized in Polynesian society (as in India, Thailand, and the Philippines) by their failure to play the central male roles of husband and father of many children. This failure puts them outside the serious arenas of politics and ceremonial activities around which prestige in Polynesia is centered (Besnier 1996). Only if the gender liminal abandons his gender nonconformity by marrying and becoming a household head can he participate as a meaningful male member of Polynesian society.

GENDER LIMINALITY AND THE POLYNESIAN
CONCEPT OF THE PERSON

Given the absence of any strongly institutionalized role for gender diversity in Polynesia, one of the significant factors that may explain its widespread (and indeed, increasing) presence is the Polynesian concept of the person. This concept focuses, as previously noted, on the importance of the social role rather than on the individual as a holistic and atomistic entity, so central to modern Euro-American culture. In Polynesia, persons are made up of different aspects, including male and female, which are foregrounded in different social contexts. Thus, gender liminality, like other aspects of a person, is highly context dependent, viewed not as indicating a kind of person but rather as a relationship between an individual and a social context. This means (as we shall see also in Thailand) that there is a gap between the social importance given to what people do in public contexts and what they do in private. Additionally, a person may be derided for some aspects of his or her character in some contexts, while praised for other aspects of his or her character or behavior in other contexts. Thus, unlike American society, where an individual's total persona may be spoiled by one stigma (Goffman 1963), in Polynesia the "person" is a multifaceted identity, and occupying a gender liminal status is not the basis of a totalizing characterization.

In contrast with gender variance among American Indians, and the ritualized homosexuality of some parts of neighboring Melanesia, neither of which "survived the moral onslaught of colonial authorities and missionaries," in Polynesia today gender diversity appears to be increasing (Besnier 1997). Whatever the traditional reasons for the emergence and maintenance of gender liminality in Polynesia, in contemporary Polynesian societies gender diversity is being realized in the contexts of the modification of traditional cultural patterns, such as the performances of fa'afafine at bridal showers, and also in entirely new patterns, such as the association of gender liminal men with foreigners in urban Polynesian bars for the purpose of sexual relations. As Besnier notes, one of the striking aspects of gender liminal persons in Polynesia is their association with innovation, their willingness to adapt, and their role in social change, an association also true of gender variants in the Philippines. In Polynesia, the gender liminal person has more than usual contact with foreigners and is frequently found in urban centers, engaged in occupations that involve him in a cash or even a global economy and in a new discourse of gender and sexuality. In this, as in other ways, he has much in common with the subjects of the next chapter, the *kathoey* of Thailand and the *bakla* of the Philippines.

Chapter Five

Transgendered Males in Thailand and the Philippines

Thailand and the Philippines share important themes regarding gender diversity. In both societies today gender diversity primarily refers to transgendered males who, by preference, take the receptor role in same-sex sexual relations and who appropriate feminine attributes and engage in feminine behavior, particularly transvestism. The **kathoey** of Thailand and the **bayot/bantut/bakla** (regionally variant names, which I use interchangeably) in the Philippines are sometimes referred to as a "third sex," but they are more widely understood to be effeminate homosexuals who are like women but also are not women. The definition of gender diversity as transgendered homosexuality in both these cultures has an important effect on social attitudes toward the kathoey and the bakla.

Both Thailand and the Philippines are characterized by multiple sex/gender discourses (Garcia 1996; Jackson 1997a; Johnson 1997; Manalansan IV 1997; Morris 1994). Both cultures have been influenced significantly by Western sex/gender ideologies, particularly the heterosexual/homosexual dichotomy, which exists alongside older and more traditional concepts. As in Brazil, in traditional Thai and Filipino cultures, sexual orientation and sexual practices were not the basis of a personal or social identity, and the modern Western opposition of homosexual/heterosexual as types of persons did not exist. Since midcentury, however, Western biomedical concepts of homosexuality and, more recently, Western concepts of "gay" identity have become part of both Thai and Filipino culture, though in different ways.

71

In Thailand and the Philippines, sex/gender diversity is significantly associated with beauty and entertainment. If gender is a performance, as modern gender theorists claim (Butler 1990), Thai and Filipino gender variants have dual gender performances: one in their everyday activities and another on the stage, which in a literal sense is an important site of the creation and enactment of sex/gender transformations.

Much Western writing about sex/gender diversity in Thailand and the Philippines portrays these societies as approving or tolerating sex/gender diversity, partly because it is highly visible. In fact, because of the overlay of Western culture, and/or the absence or bias of historical records, traditional attitudes toward sex/gender diversity are not easily reconstructed, particularly in the Philippines. In both societies, however, it is clear that historically transvestite, transgender, "third sexes," and other forms of sex/gender diversity were more accommodated than is the case today. In indigenous pre-Spanish Philippine cultures, homoeroticism was unmarked and in Thailand it was not a matter for surveillance either by the Buddhist religion or state law.

Currently in Thailand and the Philippines, however, attitudes toward gender diversity are complex and ambivalent and include hostility and ridicule. Legally, the energetic state regulation of sexuality in the West contrasts to the absence of such legislation in either Thailand or the Philippines. Socially, however, gender diversity is accepted or tolerated mainly at the margins of society, with the exception of the entertainment and beauty industries. In both cultures, the diffusion of Western biomedical models of homosexuality as inversion has negatively affected social attitudes (Garcia 1996; Jackson 1997b), though, at the same time, the Western-inspired "gay" identity has put a more favorable gloss on gender nonconformity (Manalansan IV 1997; Sullivan and Leong 1995).

THE KATHOEY OF THAILAND

Thailand's culture is closely associated with Theravada Buddhism, and much of what is known about Thai sex/gender diversity historically is based on Buddhist records. In Thai culture, biological sex, culturally ascribed gender, and sexuality are not clearly distinguished, and all three concepts are rendered by the Thai term *phet*. Historically, the Thai sex/gender pattern included an intermediate category, the kathoey, which was available to both males and females and existed alongside normative masculine and feminine identities (Jackson 1997a; 1997b).

Until the 1970s, males and females, (biological) hermaphrodites, and cross-dressing men and women could all come under the umbrella term, kathoey. Subsequently, however, the term kathoey was dropped for

cross-dressing masculine females who are now universally referred to as
tom, derived from the English "tomboy." The feminine lesbian partners
of the tom, previously not distinguished from gender-normative females,
are called *dee* (from the last syllable of lady). (For a feminist interpreta-
tion of the shift in meaning of kathoey to apply only to males, see Morris
1994). As a result of shifts in meaning, the term kathoey today is most
commonly understood as a male transgender category, which in different
contexts can refer to transvestites (cross-dressers), hermaphrodites,
transsexuals, and effeminate homosexuals (Jackson 1997b:60).

The kathoey has a long history in Thailand. Buddhist origin myths
describe three original human sex/genders—male, female, and biological
hermaphrodite or kathoey. The kathoey was *not* defined merely as a variant of male or female, but as an independently existing third sex, though
perhaps with a secondary meaning of a male who acts like a woman. This
system of three human sexes, with the kathoey as the third sex, remained
prevalent in Thailand until the mid-twentieth century.

In the 1950s, a Western "scientific" or biomedical discourse on sex
and gender was introduced into Thailand. In its Thai version, this discourse emphasized the difference between homosexuals, who were

Traditionally, kathoey referred to biological hermaphrodites, but it now refers
mainly to transgendered males. (Photograph by Ravinder Nanda.)

viewed as psychological "inverts," and kathoeys, who were viewed as biological hermaphrodites (Jackson 1997b:61). The biomedical approach implicitly continued older, Buddhist views that kathoeys were natural phenomena, whose condition was a result of karmic fate, preordained from birth and thus beyond their capacity to alter. This view is still commonly held in Thailand both by ordinary people and by kathoeys. This identification of the biomedical with the Buddhist position preserved—indeed, was developed in part to preserve—the traditional Thai ethical position regarding kathoeys: people who are different or disabled because of their karma should be pitied rather than ridiculed. The biomedical view also reinforced the Buddhist-based Thai belief that kathoeys are not sinful because their behavior is beyond their control.

HOMOEROTICISM IN THAI CULTURE

Same-sex sexual activity between masculine-identified men, called "playing with a friend" (and applied to lesbians as well), has historically been distinguished in Thailand from sex between a man and a (feminine) kathoey, whose homoeroticism was seen as rooted in biological hermaphroditism. The biomedical and the Buddhist views reinforce the popular Thai belief that cross-gender sexual relations (that is, between a kathoey and a man) are less stigmatizing than same-gender sexuality (between two masculine appearing males), because men, unlike kathoeys, are not fated to engage in this type of activity. Same-sex/gender eroticism (what would be called homosexuality in the modern West) was considered inauspicious, resulting in natural disasters, such as droughts, being struck dead by lightning, or becoming crazy. These consequences do not appear to have been directed at (heterogender) man/kathoey relationships (Jackson 1997b:63–64).

In traditional Thai sex/gender discourse, male (and female) homoeroticism was understood as sex/gender inversion or "psychological hermaphroditism," that is, having a woman's mind in a man's body. Though homoeroticism has long been recognized in Thailand, Thai culture and language did not recognize distinctive homosexual or heterosexual identities for those homoerotic males and females who in other respects adhered to normative masculine or feminine gender roles. Thus, traditionally, sexuality (same-sex sexual activity) was not central in defining the gender identities of man, woman, or kathoey. However, this has now changed.

In the last several decades, with the spread of the biomedical definition of homosexuality as inversion, homosexuality has become central in the cultural construction of the kathoey, who is now primarily considered a transgendered homosexual rather than a biological hermaphrodite (Jackson 1997a:172). Echoing a discourse about the hijras, "genuine" hermaphroditic kathoeys are distinguished from "false" or "artificial" kathoeys, who are transgendered homosexuals. This distinction continues to emphasize that the genuine kathoey has both male and female genitals. Although the older definition of kathoey as a distinctive intermediate or third sex/gender category (with no reference to sexuality) is still sometimes used in the popular media, the dominant popular stereotype of the kathoey today is that of a male who dresses and acts like a woman and who sexually relates exclusively to other males (in the receptor role) (Morris 1994; Jackson 1997a:312, fn 6).

TRANSFORMATIONS IN TRADITIONAL SEX/GENDER IDEOLOGY

In the 1970s, with the introduction of the term "gay" in Thailand, the meanings of homoeroticism changed. This resulted in a change in the meaning of the kathoey and in the structure of the Thai sex/gender system. In traditional Thailand male homoeroticism was largely ignored if it remained private. As in Brazil, insertive anal sex by a masculine appearing man did not damage his masculine identity; indeed, it might be viewed as an enjoyment of sexual variety that even enhanced masculine identity. "Feminine" sexual practices, however, specifically, taking the receptor role in anal sex, were stigmatized and if publicly known, defined a man as socially deficient and ranked him even lower than a kathoey.

When the English term gay entered Thai culture, it referred mainly to a cross-dressing or effeminate homosexual male; by the 1990s, however, the Thai image of gay became increasingly masculinized (as also occurred in Euro-American culture by the 1960s). The gay man in Thailand today is identified with gym-enlarged biceps and pectoral muscles and with accentuated body and facial hair. As newspaper and magazine personal columns demonstrate, the Thai gay confidently proclaims his identity as a man (Jackson 1995).

Self-identified gay men in Thailand are equally or even more concerned with their masculine identity than heterosexual men and model themselves on the dominant masculine image except for their sexual orientation. This masculinized gay identity, which strongly disassociates itself from the imputed feminine gender status of the kathoey, is now well established among educated and middle-class Thai male homosexuals and appears to be filtering down to the lower and working classes. Gay identity offers Thai homosexual men a new subjectivity; it now

exists alongside the category of kathoey, and both categories appear to be
growing.

The emerging gay identity in Thailand has blurred the earlier
opposition between "masculine" and "feminine" roles in same-sex erotic
practices. Traditionally, in man/kathoey sexual relations, the man penetrated the kathoey, never the reverse. In the new Thai construct of gay
identity, insertive and receptive anal sex are no longer defining markers
of gender identity, but rather are viewed as mere personal preferences.
Gay identity in Thailand is thus identified with homoerotic preference
(sexual orientation), *not* (as in Brazil) with any particular sexual practice
(i.e., active vs. passive sex role). The gay in Thailand today represents
the emergence of a third term added to the earlier structure of Thai male
sex/gender categories in which kathoey and man were positioned as
polar opposites.

Gay identity may be new in contemporary Thailand, but it refers to
an earlier, implicit, subcategory of masculine status: a man who is gender normative in all but his homoerotic preferences. Gay identity is thus
consistent with the traditional Thai concept of "man" as a sex/gender category that accommodated homoerotic preferences as simply a variation
of masculine sexuality in men who otherwise were gender normative.

In Thai popular culture today, the categories of man (which
includes gays and heterosexual men) and kathoey are viewed as polar
opposites: each category represents a constellation of sexual norms and
gender characteristics regarded as mutually exclusive. A Thai man
regards himself as either a man or a kathoey. In the modern Thai sex/
gender system the kathoey becomes the negative "other" against which
the masculine identities of both gays and men are defined (Jackson
1997a:172). The Thai gay man defines himself as a man and not as a
kathoey, rejecting all the kathoey's feminine attributes except his exclusive homosexual orientation. Together, gays, men, and kathoeys form
structurally related components of an emerging Thai sex/gender system:
each component defines and supports the construction of the other. With
the emergence of "the gay" (normally used as a noun in Thailand) as a
masculine identity, the kathoey's transgendered behavior and his feminine gender identity, along with his inverted (homo)sexuality, becomes
structurally significant, distinguishing him(her) from other males.

The sex/gender system in contemporary Thailand, then, comprises
two discrete and parallel sets of discourses. A borrowed Western system
of four sexualities, in which the homosexual/heterosexual binary crosses
the man/woman binary (see Morris 1994), has been imposed on the
indigenous system of three sex/genders—the kathoey, woman, and man.
The older system has been transformed and adjusted by the diffusion of
the newer, Western, model.

SOCIAL ATTITUDES TOWARD THE KATHOEY

As in other patriarchal cultures, like the Philippines, in Thailand the less-valued status of women stigmatizes effeminate or transgendered men. This stigma attached to the kathoey today is reinforced by the contemporary denigration of transgendered homosexuality by self-identified gay males and the larger society. This suggests that it is not same-sex sexuality per se that is stigmatizing, but rather the associated mark of femininity. Both traditionally and currently, a Thai male who dresses, talks, and acts like a Thai man and who fulfills his social obligations by marrying and fathering a family is honored by being considered a man, even if his preferred sexual partner is a male.

Unlike the West, in Thailand homoeroticism traditionally was neither condemned as sinful nor criminalized. Thai society is generally non-interventionist in sexual matters, and Thai culture (like Polynesian culture) puts a greater premium for everyone on the conventionality of one's public acts, rather than on the nonconformity of one's private emotions or behavior. Therefore, a homosexuality that does not breach other masculine gender norms need not be—and is not viewed as—a source of confrontation with society or a matter of social condemnation.

In Thailand, how one acts is more important than how one feels, and the public expression of one's "true self" is not valued as it is in the West (Morris 1994). Thus, "coming out" as a gay or a kathoey brings a "loss of face" without the compensating value of "being oneself," which is part of modern Euro-American culture. Against this Thai cultural pattern, the visibility of the kathoey becomes less rather than more valued.

On the other hand, traditionally and also in some contemporary contexts, kathoeys are "accepted." They are highly visible and found in all social strata (except at the highest levels of Thai nobility). Kathoeys live and work openly in cities, rural towns, and villages. Many perform in transvestite revues at gay bars and theaters and also participate in transvestite beauty contests, which are very popular and attended by local dignitaries, politicians, the public at large, and tourists. Thai men and women exhibit an open fascination with kathoeys; they are viewed as entertaining and humorous, and also (in contrast to the Indian attitude toward hijras, but similar to the attitude in the Philippines), associated with feminine grace, elegance, and beauty (Jackson 1997b:71).

Nevertheless, (again like in the Philippines), among upper-middle-class urbanites, kathoeys are criticized for being loud, lewd, and vulgar, particularly un-Thai-like behavior. Although many kathoeys work at ordinary jobs and also run their own businesses, they have the reputation of being sexual libertines and prostitutes, which contributes to their generally derided social position. In the past this sexual license was accepted in Thailand, possibly because the kathoey provided a "safe" sexual outlet for unmarried youth, whose sexual initiations might otherwise sully the reputation of young unmarried women (Jackson 1997a:173), a role similar to that played by transgendered males in the Philippines (Whitam 1992).

With the emergence of the gay as a masculine male, and the changing meaning of kathoey from biological hermaphrodite to transgendered homosexual, however, kathoeys face increasing social and sexual stigmatization, and even physical violence (Jackson 1997a:171). The kathoey's cross-gender persona, with its assumed permanent sexual subordination in the receptor role, now makes him a kind of "deficient male," not an independent sex/gender category. The kathoey is also derided because of his rejection of the strongly sanctioned expectation that all Thai men other than Buddhist monks should marry and become fathers.

Finally, the kathoey is increasingly derided because of his homosexuality, as this concept has been influenced by mid-twentieth-century American psychiatry. In this view, which has spread to Thai scientific/ academic discourse and the Thai upper-middle, educated classes, homosexuality is an abnormal, unnatural, category of "inversion" and of perversion.

By the 1970s and 1980s, transvestites and transsexuals were also distinguished from (biological) hermaphrodites and viewed as "false" kathoeys, who, like homosexual men, were considered to suffer from a psychological disorder. Homosexuality and male transgenderism are now considered "social problems" by Thai academics and the upper-middle classes. Attempts to "root out" these "perversions" have become part of official rhetoric, which at the same time, however, urges compassion toward homosexuals and transgenderists as individuals.

The complex and multiple discourses of the Thai sex/gender ideology, along with other Thai cultural values, challenge any oversimplified characterizations of Thai "acceptance" of sex/gender diversity. Nevertheless, sex/gender diversity has a long history in Thailand, with roots in a traditional religious culture. As in the Philippines, these echoes of a more humane and flexible past continue to influence contemporary attitudes.

SEX/GENDER DIVERSITY IN THE PHILIPPINES

Island Southeast Asia, including the Philippines, has a long tradition of highly valued male transvestite and transgendered roles (Errington 1990; Garcia 1996). Gender roles in indigenous, pre-Euro-American contact populations were generally complementary and egalitarian, and one's anatomic sex or sexual practices had little bearing on one's identity or social position. Ritual and healing roles were associated with feminine attributes and were occupied by females or transvestite males, called *babyalan*, who dressed and acted like women in order to perform their powerful and prestigious roles (Errington 1990; Garcia 1996:125ff). The same-sex sexual relationships of these men may well have followed their feminine role taking. Same-sex sexual practices were, in any case, not culturally marked and apparently irrelevant to transgendering for ritual purposes. As among American Indians, the male sexual partner of the babyalan was an ordinary man, whose same-sex sexual relations gave him no special status.

In the complex state societies of island Southeast Asia, transgendered and cross-dressed males were associated with sacred personages, were guardians of state regalia and ritual healers, and were accomplished singers and dancers who performed at various celebrations and rites of passage. In the holistic cultures of Southeast Asia (influenced by Hinduism), where the union of opposites is a central religious and political theme, transvestites and transgendered figures were metaphors for cosmic unity. As such they embodied ancestral continuity and potency, mediating between a divine world and the mundane world of human beings (Johnson 1997:12, 25). Historically, then, gender diversity in the Philippines was not relegated to the margins of society, but rather was symbolically central.

Unlike the relative continuity of Thai culture up to the present, however, the Philippines has a history of foreign domination, first by Muslim Arabs, later by Spain (from the sixteenth to the nineteenth centuries), and still later by the United States, which acquired the Philippines in 1898 as a result of the Spanish American war. An important effect of these external cultural patterns was a "sexualizing" and masculinizing of Filipino culture. From an indigenous tradition where same-sex sexual practices were unmarked and where anatomic sex was not a major determinant of prestige, the sex/gender binary of male and female acquired hierarchical dimensions. Cultural influences included an Islamic ethic emphasizing male potency and women as the embodiment of the pure and the traditional (Johnson 1997); a Catholic Spanish culture in which same-sex sexual relations, labeled sodomy, became marked and denigrated, along with the denigration of the feminine and of male transgendering; and an American scientific discourse defining homosexuality as a pathological inversion (similar to what occurred in Thailand) (Garcia 1996). More recently, as in Thailand, although with different meanings, a new, Western gay sensibility, identity, and political activism have also emerged (Manalansan IV 1995). These external cultural impositions dominate Filipino concepts of sex/gender diversity today, though older traditions have not been completely eliminated and, indeed, are being revitalized.

CONTEMPORARY CONSTRUCTIONS OF GENDER DIVERSITY: TRANSGENDERED MALE HOMOSEXUALITY

Contemporary gender diversity in the Philippines centers on male transgendering: these gender variant roles are called bakla, bantut, or bayot, depending on the region. These roles conflate effeminacy in appearance and mannerisms, transvestism, psychic inversion, and same-sex sexual relations. Bakla are males with a feminine "heart" or spirit, who cross-dress and who are assumed to take the feminine (receptor) role in sex. As with Thai and many other cultures, Filipino sex/gender ideology traditionally does not include a homosexual/heterosexual distinction in which "homosexual" refers to both partners in a same-sex sexual relationship: only the transgendered bakla is labelled homosexual. In the general stereotype, bakla are thought of as "pseudo-women" (Manalansan IV 1995:197).

The term bakla has negative connotations of indecisive, weak, or cowardly; the common stereotype also includes vulgarity and low-class status—the screaming drag queen of the 1960s Stonewall rebellion (Manalansan IV 1997). The term bantut has even stronger negative connotations in Muslim areas of the Philippines, where it denotes male impotence and a "joke of a woman," or more seriously, a defiled woman (in opposition to the purity of traditional women). Bantut are neither men nor women, and their receptor role in same-sex sexual relations is considered an abomination in Muslim culture (Johnson 1997).

Similar to the opposition of man and kathoey in Thailand, in the Philippines a "real man" is "one who is not bakla." A real man is defined as "brave" and "level headed" and by his ability to have children and sustain a family (Garcia 1996:55). Bakla also sometimes refers to a state of anatomic confusion, that is, a hermaphrodite or a physically deficient male, though there is no evidence that bakla are in fact anatomically different from other men. Because of the negative connotations of local terms for gender diversity, many bakla prefer to self-identify as gay, a term, however, that does not apply to their masculine partners and thus conveys a different meaning from that of Euro-American culture (and of Thailand as well).

A WOMAN'S HEART IN A MAN'S BODY

The bakla's core gender identity or "heart" is feminine. This identification is based on the Filipino cultural concepts of "inside" (loob) and "outside" (*labas*), a neat convergence with the Western mind/body dichotomy. The loob/labas distinction emphasizes that the identity of all persons—man, woman, or other—is largely based on an inner, subjective reality (the loob), which guides, affirms, or countervails external appearance (the labas). In one part of the Philippines, for example, the term bayot literally translates as "a woman with a penis," an expression that privileges the inner reality of femininity against the outward appearance as a genital (anatomic) male (Garcia 1998, citing Hart, p. 55).

For the bakla themselves, their inversion consists of a woman's heart, spirit, or psyche in a male body, a concept consistent with the Western inversion model of homosexuality in which the individual's psychological being is opposite to his/her anatomy. Unlike the Filipino opposition of loob/labas, however, which privileges the spirit, the Western concept of inversion privileges the body as the standard against which the psychic opposition becomes "abnormal."

BAKLA SEXUAL RELATIONSHIPS

While same-sex sexual relations of the bakla is only one factor (and perhaps not even the most important) in his social construction, the bakla's sexuality is important in his subjective identity and also affects social attitudes toward him. The Western categorical and sexual separation of homosexuals from heterosexuals contrasts with the high degree of sexual interaction between bakla and non-bakla in the Philippines. It is very common in the Philippines for adolescent boys and young adults, who will later marry heterosexually and fully engage in maintaining families, to have sex for money with bakla (in some cities this involves perhaps 75 percent of young, working-class males [Whitam 1992]). These males, referred to as "callboys," like the maridos of Brazilian travestís, are not marked as homosexuals by society and do not experience themselves as such. The Filipino view that only the "feminine" partner in the sexual relationship is a homosexual reinforces the emphasis on the feminine loob as the core of bakla identity.

Masculine-appearing men, who are assumed to take the inserter sexual position, are also assumed to have a masculine loob; they are thus real men even as they have sexual relations with bakla. In spite of the fact that callboys or male partners of the bakla acknowledge sexual satisfaction as well as monetary benefits from their bakla relationships, the masculine-appearing partner stoutly denies any deep affection or emotional impact in the relationship. The social stereotype holds that only the feminine bakla is deeply emotionally affected by these sexual relationships.

Inversion theory (in both its Filipino and Western biomedical versions) presumes that only one partner in a same-sex sexual relation is an invert; thus in both Thailand and the Philippines, it is the transgendered male, who is assumed also to play the "feminine" or receptor role in sex, who has become "the homosexual." Like Brazilian travestís, Filipino bakla say that to penetrate a man transforms the penetrated man into a woman. They explicitly reject the possibility that they could accept a man who wishes to be penetrated by them as their boyfriend. Among the bakla, then, as in the society at large, a man who desires penetration loses his masculine identity.

Bakla conform to the "heterogender" nature of sexual relationships dominant in the Philippines: they explicitly state that sexual relations between two bakla do not occur and is repulsive. In some regions of the Philippines, two bayot having sex with each other is considered "incest" or "eating their own flesh" (Garcia 1996:97). Bakla sexual relationships across the genders means that for many bakla, their feminine identity centers on their exclusive sexual and romantic interests in "real" men. More specifically, many bakla define themselves as women in terms of their wish to be penetrated by a "real" man (Johnson 1997:90). This is consistent with the cultural understanding of the bakla's femininity as a marker of their "inverted" sexuality. Many bakla say that their first experience of anal penetration, however violently imposed, confirmed their transgendered identity in their own eyes (Johnson 1997), a self-characterization also expressed by Brazilian travestí (Kulick 1998).

Bakla typically express their desire for a real man as deep longing; they experience themselves as having the "weaker" emotions of women, an image based on sexual desire as shaped by the gender hierarchy and the view that women, like the Virgin Mary (a powerful image in Catholic Filipino culture), were meant to suffer for men. It is this imitation of the stereotypical female in a patriarchal culture that is at the core of the bakla role (Manalansan IV 1995:197). Bakla acknowledge that however sexually desirable they are, the mutuality of their relationships with real men are limited because they cannot bear children. Thus, they feel doomed to suffer in their love relationships no matter how feminine and subservient they are (Cannell 1995:241).

Yet, paradoxically, bakla, like hijras, travestís, and Polynesian gender variants, also are viewed as sexual aggressors. In addition, as pointed out by Don Kulick (1998) for the travestí, the material benefits the bakla confer on their partners also gives them a certain leverage and source of control in these relationships (Manalansan IV, personal communication 1999). Thus, bakla, like travestís, hijras, and māhūs, are by no means merely victims in unequal sexual relationships.

THE ASSOCIATION OF TRANSGENDERED
MALES WITH BEAUTY

Beauty in the Philippines is associated with successful performance, which includes, in a very central way, the ability to transform
oneself successfully from one's ordinary role. The aim is less to "pass" as
what one is not than to act convincingly in a role temporarily, through
dress and other appropriations. The bakla, as males who display a highly
successful ability to present themselves as women within certain contexts, are therefore closely associated with the concept of beauty in their
own eyes and in the eyes of society (Cannell 1995:242; 1999). This trans-
formative ability is expressed in their specialized occupations in fashion,
entertainment, hairstyling and beauty salons and particularly in their
participation in beauty contests.

Bakla identity, formed around the "inside/outside structure" of the
loob and the labas, calls for the loob—the inside, immaterial female
spirit—to be "exposed" by inscribing feminine beauty on the body, the
most concrete site of the expression of the loob (Johnson 1997:90). Bakla
beauty is understood as bodily practices aimed at style, glamour, and
femininity. In defining themselves as feminine, bakla/bantut emphasize
the care they give their bodies, their concern with cleanliness and beauty,
their use of facial creams and body lotion to "soften" their bodies, their
wearing makeup, jewelry, and perfume, and their cross-dressing
(Johnson 1997). The importance of beauty to transgendered identities
emerges in bantut life-histories, particularly in the notion of "exposure"
(Johnson 1997:124). For many bantut, "coming out," which usually
occurs in high school or college, is expressed as "exposing my beauty."
Bantut commonly greet each other by asking, "How is your beauty?"
instead of "How are you?" This emphasis on bodily appearance is consistent with the Philippine cultural understanding of the body as an important site for self-transformation. Thus, the bantut are not merely imitating women but are "capturing" the power of femininity through beauti-
fying their bodies and through their gender transformations.

TRANSVESTITE BEAUTY CONTESTS

In the Philippines, transformations of various kinds are associated
with power (Cannell 1995; 1999). Positive social attitudes toward bakla
are largely based on their ability to transform themselves into glamour-
ous and stylish women. In transvestite beauty contests, bakla transform
themselves by conveying a highly valued, global, and cosmopolitan

image of glamour and style identified with the West, particularly America, and in the Philippines associated with the upper-class, educated elite and celebrities, themselves shaped by Western culture.

The most visible and compelling sites for the presentation of transgendered beauty are transvestite beauty contests, which are a growing phenomenon in Southeast Asia and the Pacific (Cohen et al. 1996). The audiences include bakla and straight people, and the contests are considered perfectly suitable family affairs. Local dignitaries, village businesspeople, members of local leader families, and men, women and children all attend.

Beauty contests give status and pleasure to the bakla, some of whom have an obsession with participating as a way of "exposing" their beauty. Most of the contests are organized around international themes, illustrated by names like Miss Gay World or Miss Gay International, which emphasize bakla identification with the powerful global "otherness" of America (Cannell 1995). The contests may even be a re-emergence of traditional ritual transvestite roles as mediating figures, though today instead of mediating between the divine and the mundane, the bakla mediate between the local and global culture (Cannell 1999; Johnson 1996:90; Peacock 1987).

Points in the beauty contests are awarded for beauty, such as "Best in Evening Gown" and "Miss Photogenic," but more than half the points are based on "intelligence," exemplified in the question-and-answer portion of the contest. The questions, which are asked and must be answered in English, relate to topics like politics and careers (Johnson 1996), again emphasizing a cosmopolitan, Western source of prestige. Though the material rewards of winning the contest are small, contestants take the contests very seriously. There is also an underlying comic tension; the audience applauds genuine intelligence and beauty, but there are also catcalls and glee when the "beauty" becomes unglued, as in a broken heel or a slippage of costume. Most contestants wear very tight underwear and full length stockings. They tape or tie their genitals between their thighs, and there is always anticipation that the male will emerge accidentally from the female, an occasion for laughter that is not always compassionate.

The Americanized images of beauty in the contests are closely linked to the early-twentieth-century American colonial regime. The American mandate emphasized American-style education aimed particularly at transforming Filipinos into participating citizens of a modern, democratic state. Today schools and educators are among the predominant sponsors not only of the beauty contests (which are mostly organized by bakla) but of the many other contests and performances (such as talent shows and sports contests) that are part of American civic culture, which emphasizes discipline, self-development, and self-respect. As the question-and-answer portion of the beauty contests most clearly demonstrates, beauty is significantly about education, mastery of English, good citizenship, a professional career orientation, and democratic fair play, as well as glamour. In short, "beauty" is articulated by and associated with those institutions identified with the "knowledge power" of the Americans, and beauty is a primary idiom within which this "global other" is identified.

Although the association of bakla with the creation and presentation of this international concept of beauty is a source of power, it is also a source of ambivalence, particularly in the Muslim areas of the south. In these areas bantut identification with the global "other" generates ambivalence. The Muslims continually and actively resisted both Spanish and American domination. Within this context, the Muslim masculine ideal became closely associated with aggressive militarism and the feminine ideal with maintaining purity—both sexual and cultural—in opposition to external domination. Thus, in Muslim-dominated areas, bantuts are not only gender "deviants"—as neither men nor women—but ethnic deviants as well. To the extent that the West (and its affiliation with the Christian Filipino state) is perceived as a threat to local Muslim culture, power, and identity, bantuts' identification with this external culture lowers their status. The positively valued "exposure" of bantut beauty turns into negatively valued "overexposure" (to the West) and undermines bantut acceptance in local communities (Johnson 1997).

During the 1970s, bakla unsuccessfully attempted to improve their social position by identifying themselves as a "third" sex/gender (*sward*), in an attempt (like the one in Europe in the late-nineteenth century) to "naturalize" their sex/gender nonconformity and thus make it "equal" to the sex/gender of males and females, men and women (Garcia 1996:197). But because in the Philippines, same-sex sexual behavior is transformed through the concept of inversion into heterogender behavior and modeled on it, the "thirdness" of the bakla had little impact on their social status. Although the bakla and their sex/gender transformations are the "stars" of spectacular performances, these performances perhaps do more to contain gender diversity than promote it. Like the Euro-American transsexual, bakla transgendering may do more to confirm a binary sex/gender system than to undermine it, reinforcing rather than mitigating their marginality in society.

Chapter Six

Sex/Gender Diversity in Euro-American Cultures

The contemporary Euro-American view that there are only two sexes and two genders and that the distinctions between male and female, man and woman, are natural, unchangeable, universal, and desirable is reflected in both popular culture and the biological and social sciences (Herdt 1996a). Apart from a small group of scholars and gender variants themselves, this dichotomy is so firmly in place that it has largely erased the historical knowledge of alternatives—sex/gender ideologies that incorporated several models of sex/gender diversity.

It has been persuasively argued that a one-sex model, that of "a male/masculine body and mind inscribed on the incomplete and subordinate female body," has roots in European antiquity and persisted up until the Middle Ages (Laqueur 1990). In ancient Greece one- and two-gender models existed side by side. Aristotle, for example, although rooted in the Greek gender ideology of binary opposites, nevertheless conceptualized a one-gender model in his view of sexuality as an ascending ladder of perfection. Women and girls were at the bottom of the ladder; part way up were boys and adolescent males; and at the top were aristocratic men (see Bullough 1993:46). The one-sex model is also implied in the Genesis story, in which Adam creates Eve from his own loins. In Plato's *Symposium*, however, Aristophanes argues that three sexes were part of an original human nature: "man, woman, and the union of the two . . . having a double nature . . ." (Buchanan 1977:143).

Other models of sex/gender diversity emerged in different historical periods. In the sixteenth and seventeenth centuries, northern European culture identified three sexes—male, female, and hermaphrodite—and two genders—man and woman (Trumbach 1996). All three biological sexes were assumed capable of having sexual relations with males and females, though each was ordinarily presumed to have sexual relations only with the opposite gender. It was believed that those born biologically intersexed could change their gender, but if hermaphrodites continually switched their gender and took sexual partners of both genders, they were treated as having committed the crime of sodomy. The interests of the state and the church in upholding the dominant hierarchical and patriarchal sex/gender system was a key factor in European attitudes toward sex/gender diversity, hence the prosecution of intersexed gender switchers.

By the late-seventeenth century, concepts of gender diversity centered on the relationship between male same-sex sexual practices and cross-gender behavior. Up until the early-1700s adult men who engaged in sexual relations with both men and women suffered no loss in their masculine gender status because the predominant form of these relationships, in which adult men sexually penetrated younger boys, did not violate the hierarchical, patriarchal gender code that governed relations between men and women (Trumbach 1998). But adult men who allowed themselves to be penetrated (a subordinate position associated with women) and who exhibited some feminine behaviors were classified in the stigmatized gender variant category of hermaphrodite. In this premodern period, male hermaphroditism was viewed as a quality of the mind, and did not refer, as it does today, to biological or anatomical qualities.

The term hermaphrodite as applied to women also signified gender infractions such as wearing masculine-looking clothing, but did not necessarily imply same-sex sexual desire, as it did for men. But women who desired women, especially if they dressed or acted like men, were believed to be anatomical hermaphrodites (in contrast to the psychological hermaphroditism of males) and were often medically examined for evidence of masculine biology, such as an enlarged clitoris (Trumbach 1996).

Sex/gender diversity, then, was associated with sexual object choice and cross-gender behavior. Although at this time male gender variants were called hermaphrodites and not homosexuals, the association between same-sex sexual desire and effeminacy continued in various forms well into the twentieth century.

By around 1700, when the acceptance of age-structured same-sex sexual relations among males declined, male same-sex sexual desire became associated with the social role of the *molly*, which was considered a third gender category, albeit an illegitimate one. The molly was an effeminate man whose sexual preference as an adult was to take the passive sexual role with adult male partners; somewhat later the role of the *sapphist*—a woman who preferred female sexual partners—emerged. The two "illegitimate" genders of the molly (or sodomite) and the sap-

Historically, in Euro-American cultures, male homosexuality was associated with effeminacy and gender variance. This group of gay police officers in the New York City gay pride march demonstrates how this concept has changed. (Photograph by Serena Nanda.)

phist were added to the two legitimate genders of man and woman, resulting in a system of four genders and two sexes (male and female). By 1800, gender was firmly defined by sexuality: masculine and feminine gender roles included sexual desire for the opposite gender, while sodomites and sapphists were defined by their sexual preferences for members of their own sex, in conjunction with other cross-gender behaviors. Male desire for another male and the associated effeminacy was viewed as a result of the "corruption" of an individual's mind that had occurred in his early experience, not as a result of any anatomical or biological deficiencies (Trumbach 1996).

By the mid-nineteenth century, Darwinian evolution and Victorian culture combined to shape a European sex/gender ideology that emphasized the opposition of two sexes—male and female—and two genders—man and woman—as functional for the reproduction and survival of the species. The Darwinian emphasis on complementary roles in reproduction rigidified the differences between male and female as innate and far ranging and cemented the definition of "normal" sexuality as the attraction of opposites. Within this framework some sexual reformers and scientific sexologists constructed homosexuality as a third, intermediate gender role in attempt to "naturalize" it, and thus undermine public hostility

(Hekma 1996). Homosexuality was seen as "a kind of interior androgyny, a hermaphroditism of the soul" (Foucault, cited in Herdt 1996a:77), an inversion consisting of "a female soul enclosed in a male body."

The association of homosexuality with gender inversion was widely accepted by the emerging profession of psychiatry, though it was rejected by many homosexuals at the time who argued that same-sex sexual practice was not only associated with masculinity, but even with a heightened virility. Nevertheless, the theory of homosexuality as sexual inversion remained firmly in place until the mid-twentieth century and, as noted earlier, later spread to non-Western societies. The construction of homosexuals as a third gender did not, however, accomplish the aims of its advocates. Under the influence of Darwinian dimorphism—the Victorian identification of masculinity with desire for the opposite sex and the psychiatric characterization of inversion as pathology (see Bullough 1993:213ff)—the categorization of homosexuals as a third, intermediate category did little to help their public image. Indeed, the association of homosexuality with effeminacy impeded popular acceptance of homosexuals who were now doubly stigmatized, once by the shame of their "abnormal" sexual leanings and second by their lowered status as women (Hekma 1996). Only after the 1960s did same-sex sexual practices break loose from their associations with cross-gender behavior and cross-gender identity, as this applied to both males and females.

Although European culture focused on male gender variance, female gender variants appear throughout European (and American) history. While some female gender variant roles, such as the sapphist of eighteenth-century London, were at least partly defined by their sexual attraction for other women, other European female gender variants were defined (as the sādhin in India), by their renunciation of sexuality. Two examples are the transvestite female saints of the Middle Ages and the "sworn virgin" of the Balkans.

TRANSVESTITE FEMALE SAINTS

In early modern European society (beginning in the early-1700s), many cases came to light of women who dressed and passed as men in order to engage in male occupations, particularly as soldiers and sailors, from which they otherwise would be barred. Such women were generally stigmatized for subverting the normal gender order and if found out in their "deceits" (which frequently involved marrying a woman under false pretenses) were tried and punished in court.

But in the Middle Ages, one kind of transvestite female had gained cultural approval. Despite the biblical injunction in Deuteronomy against wearing clothes of the opposite sex, transvestite female saints

were a significant historical fact and the stuff of legend, fulfilling the
words of St. Jerome that "a woman who wishes to serve Christ more than
the world . . . will cease to be a woman and will be called a man" (Garber
1992:214; Gregg 1997:151). Among the many female transvestite saints
was Pelagia, said to have been a prostitute who changed her ways, con-
verted to Christianity, changed her name to (the male) Pelagius, and
dressed as a man, wearing a hair shirt beneath her male clothing. Only
her death revealed her to be a woman (Bullough 1993:52).

St. Eugenia, like other female transvestite saints, cross-dressed in
order to join an all-male religious community. She later became an abbot,
and only when she was accused of rape by a rich lady who desired her,
did she reveal herself as a woman. Theodora, wife of a rich Alexandrite,
was another transvestite holy woman. Falsely accused of adultery by a
young man whose sexual advances she rejected, Theodora shaved her
head, dressed in male clothing and entered a monastery as a monk. Here
she was again falsely accused, this time by a maidservant whose sexual
advances she rejected. Theodora was expelled from the abbey, but upon
her death her true sex was revealed by angels and she was reinstated as
a subject of religious devotion (Gregg 1997:149–50).

A striking aspect of some female transvestite saints were that they
were said to be bearded (Garber 1992:214). One of the most prominent
was St. Wilgefortis, who wished to remain a virgin and devote herself to
a contemplative life but whose father insisted on her marrying the King
of Sicily. Wilgefortis's prayer for deliverance was answered by the sudden
growth of a long moustache and beard. When the Sicilian King noticed
these (in spite of her veiling), he rejected her and her father had her cru-
cified. In England St. Wilgefortis is the patron saint of married women
who wish to be rid of their husbands.

While psychoanalytical interpretations of these stories, particularly
as they involve false accusations of sexuality, have to do with the fanta-
sies of the clerics who told them (see Anson 1974), they exhibit a common
feature of patriarchal society, which sanctioned cross-dressing for women,
who thereby gained higher status, but not for men, who thereby lost status (Bullough 1993:52). As Marjorie Garber (1992) points out, there were
no cross-dressed male saints. From a more subjective perspective, a common pattern in the lives of transvestite female saints was their gender
crossing during a moment of personal crisis, marking a break with a
former existence. This pattern fits the most famous cross-dressed saint,
Joan of Arc, who like her transvestite models of the Christian monastic
tradition broke with her parents, refused to marry the husband they had
chosen for her, and "rejected male domination even as she assumed male
privilege" (Garber 1992:215). Although sharing many features with other
transvestite saints, St. Joan was more of a true gender variant in that she
did not try to pass as a man but rather insisted that she was a woman in

men's clothes. Her transvestism, which was the source of her "subversive" strength, was considered an abomination by the church and was the act for which she was put on trial. As one of her interpreters phrases it, "[St. Joan] was usurping a man's function but shaking off the trammels of his sex altogether to occupy a different, third order, neither male nor female, like the angels" (cited in Garber 1992:216).

THE SWORN VIRGIN OF THE BALKANS

Similar in some ways to the gender crossing of transvestite saints were the *sworn virgins* of the Balkans. Biological females, wearing men's dress and sometimes carrying male weapons, engaging in men's occupations and recognized as men, have been reported in the western Balkans since the early-nineteenth century (Gremaux 1996). Basically a peasant farming and pastoral region, the western Balkans had a harsh warrior culture involving continuous blood feuds and intergroup killing. Women had few rights, and because society was organized into corporate localized patrilineages, they remained social outsiders throughout their lives. Because women were unarmed, however, they were considered inviolable from assault.

Within this context (and in some places perhaps related to a shortage of males), an institutionalized form of gender crossing emerged in which female sworn virgins assumed a male social identity with the tacit approval of their families and the larger community. The sworn virgin or "manlike woman" vowed to abstain from matrimony and motherhood and to lead a virginal life. She was sometimes called "she who stays," referring to her choice to remain in her natal home and become the heir for a family that had no sons (in contrast to the normal patrilocal pattern where a wife lives with her husband's patrilineage). Violation of chastity by a sworn virgin could bring death by stoning.

Rene Gremaux (1996) describes one such female gender crosser: Tonë, a sworn virgin who lived into the mid-twentieth century, and whose life exhibited some of the common patterns of this role. Tonë was the first child of a couple who later had two sons, both of whom died in childhood. Because she had no brothers, at age nine Tonë decided to become her parents' son, with her parents' approval. She promised never to marry and began to wear boys' clothing; she retained her female name, though she/he was referred to with the male pronoun. Instead of women's tasks, Tonë helped his father with male tasks and received weapons from his father at the age of fifteen. Over the years Tonë's voice, posture, and manner of speaking changed so that it was hard to distinguish him from a biological male.

Tonë played the full gamut of male roles and was recognized and honored as a man in his community. He took care of and protected his younger sisters and a younger brother born to his parents late in life. When his sisters married, Tonë, as the older brother, handed them over to their grooms. During World War II, Tonë commanded an all-male fighter unit resisting Communist control. He was subsequently captured and much to his dismay was treated as a woman for the year he remained in prison. Upon his release he set up a communal household (away from his area of birth) with his younger brother and acted as "master of the house," receiving guests and participating in traditional all-male gatherings. Outdoors he performed only male tasks, like the heavy and prestigious work of mowing and stacking hay. Although he cooked, he did not engage in women's handicrafts. He also sang "mountaineer songs" and played the lute, traditionally male activities that became a specialty of many Albanian sworn virgins. Tonë was buried with the blessings of the Catholic Church as a virgin and in a male costume, as he requested, although he was denied the last honors of a man: the rules of the tribe in the area in which he lived did not allow a biological female to be lamented with the traditional funeral oration by males.

Rene Gremaux (1996:268) explains the gender variant of the sworn virgin as growing out of a strongly male-dominated culture in which the disappearance of the "house" without any sons was a distressing and stigmatizing event. In these patriarchal cultures (as in the medieval church), virginity was synonymous with the male virtues of purity and strength. Also, like the Indian sādhin, the sworn virgin role prevented children from being born out of wedlock, who would have no legitimate place within a patrilineal social organization in which children were believed to "spring from the blood of the father." While the sexuality of many sworn virgins was not known, the fear of pregnancy very likely restrained their heterosexual relationships, and it is possible that some were sexually attracted to other women.

In the Balkans (as in India), where women are expected to marry and become dependent on men, female adult virginity is a gender anomaly—a "problem" that can be "solved" by constructing virgin adult women as social males. Clearly, though, the main function of this institutionalized third gender role was to enable the maintenance of a patrilineal and patrilocal society by channeling female gender nonconformity and by providing the availability of an heir where there was no son. Sworn virgins inherited real estate (denied to married women, widows, and divorcees) and were expected to safeguard the family property, handing it down to appropriate male heirs. Although most sworn virgins reacted defensively to any reference to their femaleness, in some ways their female sex/gender status was acknowledged: although sworn virgins were permitted to carry arms, a man who killed or injured one intentionally was looked down upon. Rather than merely a gender crosser, the sworn virgin of the Balkans appears to be an example of that culturally "creative bricolage" which is the essential criteria of sex/gender diversity.

TRANSSEXUALISM

Cultures vary in their response to the "problem" of people with sex/gender anomalies—individuals who do not fit into either of the two sex/gender categories, or who wish to be of a sex and gender class different from that which is consistent with their anatomy. In Euro-American culture, the solution to this dilemma was the invention of the *transsexual*. Robert Stoller, a leading authority on transsexualism, defines it as "the conviction of a biologically normal person of being a member of the opposite sex" (cited in Kessler and McKenna 1978:115), a definition that admits no possibility of a third, alternative gender. In Euro-American culture, then, the transsexual is only a transitional status: a person is a transsexual when s/he is in a temporary, in-between sex status, moving from one sex to the other. The reconstructive genital surgery that transsexuals desire aims at moving them from just such a transitional, in-between state to the status of a real man or woman, a status ultimately confirmed by surgically constructed sex organs of the opposite sex.

The term "gender identity" was critical in meeting the cultural challenge presented by people born as males who want to be women, or people born as females who want to be men. Gender identity refers to the inner psychological conviction of an individual that he or she is either a man or a woman. Drawing on the mind/body split central in Western culture, gender identity is viewed as a quality of the mind—or the soul—distinguished from the body. The concept of gender identity permits society to retain the view (some would say illusion) that gender is dichotomous and permanent, even if sex can be changed (Shapiro 1991). The concept of gender identity permits the conflict experienced by transsexuals to be understood as a discordance between anatomy and subjectively experienced gender: the male or female organs are viewed as "merely" a mistake that must be corrected.

A sex-change operation offers a way of relieving the ambiguity in a sex/gender system based on binary opposites (Kessler and McKenna 1978). The reconstructive genital surgery that transsexuals desire aligns their anatomy with their gender identity. The new male or female sex status is then supported by the construction of a revised life story and certain legal changes, such as revising one's sex on the birth certificate. Through this sex change, the transsexual upholds the status quo of the binary sex/gender system.

Psychological professionals, who were central in the transsexual labeling process, were critical in defining a transsexual as a woman (or man) trapped in the body of a man (or woman) (Bolin 1988). This definition, diffused in the media, became part of the popular culture, confirmed by transsexual autobiographies. Contrary to this picture of a transsexual who has *always* experienced him- or herself as a person of the opposite sex/gender, however, are ethnographic data on transsexuals that indicate that they do not begin the process of sex transformation with fully formed identities of the opposite gender (Bolin 1996a:449). Rather (like hijras [Nanda 1996]), transsexuals gradually acquire transformed identities as they become involved in transsexual groups and go through the process of sex change. Anne Bolin (1988), in her ethnographic studies of male-to-female transsexuals, identifies this transformation as a rite of passage. In rites of passage, which are known in almost all societies, an individual moves from one status to another. For the male transsexual, there is a gradual movement from a partial and perhaps ambivalent feminine identity to an identity as a transsexual and, finally, to an identity as a complete woman. These gender identity changes are accompanied by gender role changes, as the individual moves from outwardly occupying a male role while secretly dressing as a woman; to more frequently dressing as a

The sign says it all: transsexuals move from one sex to the opposite sex. (Photograph by Serena Nanda.)

woman, perhaps passing as a woman in public; to occupying the roles of both man and woman, while increasingly passing as a woman; to the final social identity transformation into full-time status as a woman. At each stage, a parallel gradual transformation takes place as the biological male is feminized by hormones and finally, with sex-change surgery and surgical construction of a vagina, achieves full womanhood—in its psychological, behavioral, and physical dimensions (Bolin 1996a:450).

In the 1960s through the 1980s, for many male transsexuals in the United States, this process was monitored by psychological and medical professionals at prestigious, university-affiliated gender clinics that were connected with hospitals where most transsexual surgery was performed. Thus, these professionals became the "gatekeepers" of gender crossing in the United States. Most of these clinics offered services only for male-to-female transsexuals. As part of the decision that transsexual surgery was the proper therapy for individuals who presented gender identity problems, these clinics treated preoperative transsexuals with hormones and psychological counseling for two years before permitting them to undergo sex-change surgery (Shapiro 1991). Individuals who expressed ambivalence or confusion about their gender identity might be disqualified for surgery.

Male transsexuals needed to convince the mental-health professionals that they had experienced themselves as women from an early age, as far back as they could remember. They also had to demonstrate that they could live full-time as women and be accepted socially as women. This evidence supported a clinical evaluation that an individual was indeed a transsexual (and not "merely" a heterosexual transvestite or a homosexual female impersonator, conditions for which transsexual surgery was considered counterproductive). Because most medical and mental-health specialists were committed to a conventional view of the Western sex/gender dichotomy and its associated gender roles, their monitoring process contributed to the stereotypically defined femininity that research indicates most transsexuals exhibit.

In clinical practice and within the male transsexual community, transsexuals viewed themselves as authentic women, in opposition to gay female impersonators, for example, whom they saw as only "playing at" being women. Transsexuals also distinguished themselves from heterosexual cross-dressers (clinically designated transvestites) who did not have a "real" feminine identity and only cross-dressed for purposes of sexual satisfaction. For male transsexuals, the desire for bodily change became the hallmark of authentic feminine gender identity, a desire that rested on, and furthered, the Euro-American association of gender with biological sex. Transsexuals, then, far from being an example of gender diversity, both reflected and reinforced the dominant Euro-American sex/gender ideology in which one had to choose to be either a man or a (stereotypical) woman.

Transsexualism also reflected and reinforced the Euro-American cultural view that genitals were the defining feature of gender: in Western culture, gender attribution is genital attribution (Kessler and McKenna 1978). In spite of the many other "invisible" determinants of biological sex now known (chromosomes, hormones), it is the genitals as the *visible* indicators of sex that make them so important in gender identity and presentation, hence the emphasis on surgery by both medical and mental-health professionals as well as by transsexuals themselves, an emphasis that reproduces the "biological imperative of Euro-American sex/gender ideology" (Bolin 1996a:454, 455).

Transsexualism has been largely a male phenomenon, partly because female-to-male sex reassignment surgery developed much later than male-to-female sex reassignment surgery and is generally less aesthetically and surgically effective (Lothstein 1983:6–7). But this in itself may be an artifact of a male-dominated culture in which male gender dysfunction creates more anxiety than female gender dysfunction and is a problem society is more willing to solve (Garber 1992:103). The emphasis on male transsexualism also results from the different social pressures on gender conformity: it is easier for female (preoperative) transsexuals as masculine women than it is for male preoperative transsexuals with a female gender identity to adapt to a male-oriented society. Furthermore, because it is—or was, certainly until midcentury—considered natural by the psychiatric profession in patriarchal Euro-American societies for women to wish to become men, women's desires for sex transformations did not seem as indicative of a severe *psychological* disorder and therefore were not as clinically urgent as men's (Lothstein 1983:6–7). If females are not as numerically well represented as men within the transsexual category, however, they play a prominent role in the emerging phenomenon of transgenderism.

TRANSGENDERISM

The picture of transsexualism described above dominated the 1960s, 1970s, and 1980s in Europe and the United States. In the last ten years, a new concept tentatively called *transgenderism* has emerged. Transgenderism is both an individual and collective phenomenon—individuals begin to experience new sex/gender identities and individual transgendered voices become part of a new movement. Transgenderism has its foundation in the ancient tradition of **androgyny**, a view that has made the crosscultural data from anthropology—with its descriptions of the positive value of androgyny in some other cultures—particularly rel-

Gender mixing, whether
seriously or in play, pro-
vokes reflection on the culturally constructed nature
of sex and gender roles.
(Photograph by Serena
Nanda.)

evant to the transgender community (Bolin 1996b:39; Connor 1993; Feinberg 1996).

Unlike transsexuals, transpeople (transgenderists) do not consider
themselves limited to a choice of one of two genders. Transgenderism
includes a continuum of options, from individuals who wish to undergo
sex reassignment surgery to those who wish to live their lives androgynously. The previous split between transsexuals and "part-time" gender
crossers who did not wish sex reassignment surgery has been mooted to
some extent by transgenderism, which validates a range of gender roles
and identities within society and even within an individual.

Although transgenderists can be narrowly defined as persons who
want to change gender roles without undergoing sexual reassignment
surgery, but who also do not identify as "transvestites," they can also be
defined as "persons who steer a middle course, living with the physical,

social, and psychological traits of both genders." Thus, transgenderism is an inclusive term describing those "who may alter their anatomy with hormones or surgery" but also those who intentionally retain many of the characteristics of the gender to which they were originally assigned. Many transpeople lead part-time lives in both genders; most cultivate an androgynous appearance (Bolin 1996a:466).

Transgender identities vary widely, but the philosophy of transgenderism is well summarized in the words of one transperson who says: ". . . you no longer have to fit into a box . . . it is okay to be transgendered. You can now lay anywhere on the spectrum from non-gendered to full transsexual" (Bolin 1996a:475). Transgenderists view gender and sex categories, or "boxes," as improperly imposed by society and its "sexual identity gatekeepers" referred to above. Unlike transsexuals of the 1970s and 1980s, transgenderists today challenge and stretch the boundaries of the American bipolar system of sex/gender oppositions and renounce the American definition of gender as dependent on a consistency of genitals, body type, identity, role behaviors, and sexual orientation. Indeed, transgenderists reject any society's attempts to circumscribe an individual's identity and capabilities by what a culture deems to be masculine or feminine behavior (Feinberg 1996).

INTERSEXUALITY

One result of transgenderism is a revisiting of biological *intersexuality* (the condition of having ambiguous genitalia [Dreger 1998; Fausto-Sterling 1993; Kessler 1998]). Generally speaking, medical and psychological opinion holds that gender identity is learned early, that it is permanent once learned, and that a gender identity consistent with one's anatomy is a basic condition for adult mental health (see Money and Ehrhardt 1972). As a result of these assumptions, medical practice holds that sex assignment should be as early as possible, in infancy or early childhood, and that surgical intervention is recommended to shape the intersexed infant into a boy or a girl.

The value of such medical alterations in anatomy has now become a subject of debate, both in the popular culture and in the scientific community (Dreger 1998). In 1997, for example, members of the Intersex Society of North America lobbied Congress to extend a recent federal ban on genital cutting, aimed mainly at African cultural practices of cliterodectomy, to American pediatric surgeons who customarily reduce or remove infant clitorises deemed "abnormally" large, a practice affecting about 2,000 babies a year (Angier 1997:C1). The issues in the debate are about who has the right to decide what are aesthetically acceptable genitalia, whose interests are served by surgical intervention, and whether sex/gender identity is so intertwined with the appearance of the genitals that it is worth subjecting infants or children to this operation. Some persons who have experienced this surgery maintain that the negative effects (for example, a lack of clitoral sensation) are not worth the aesthetic results. As with much else in the sex/gender system, social institutions, such as the medical profession, act as gatekeepers of the Euro-American sex/gender dichotomy, in this case by surgically "normalizing" anomalous individuals at birth (Kessler 1998).

The ways that transsexuality and intersexuality are managed by the medical and psychological professions illuminates Euro-American beliefs regarding gender and genitals. Yet these beliefs, like those in any culture, are subject to change, as we have seen with the emergence of transgenderism, which involved several key factors. One was the diversity of cross-gender identities and the variety of combinations of gender identity and sexual orientations experienced within the male-to-female transsexual and transvestite populations in the United States, which contradicted the rigid differentiations psychological professionals made between transsexuals, effeminate homosexuals, and heterosexual cross-dressers (Bolin 1996a:461).

According to Anne Bolin, this diversity had always existed but was masked by the institutional requirements of the sex-change profession. The closing of the university gender clinics affiliated with hospitals doing sex-reassignment surgery permitted new, more variable social constructions of gender diversity to emerge. Private sites for sex-reassignment surgery are more "client centered" and less subject to professional "gatekeeper" decisions about who is psychologically appropriate for such surgery. In addition, in the milieu of identity politics, which has characterized the American social scene in the last 15 years, the organization of transgenderists, intersexuals, and other gender variants has found fertile ground for expansion.

Although sex-change operations achieved the personal desires of transsexuals to become members of the "opposite" sex, in aim and in result, transsexualism upheld rather than challenged the "two-party" sex/gender system of Euro-American culture. But within the transsexual pheonomenon were the seeds of transgenderism. Transsexualism began the destabilization of the necessary connection between gender and anatomy, and undermined the cultural assumption that the four elements of a sex/gender system—biology, culture, sexuality, and personal identity—were inextricably linked. From these small seeds of doubt, transgenderism may grow to present the most potentially "subversive" challenge yet to the cultural pattern of a binary sex and gender system.

Chapter Seven

Variations on a Theme

There are many cultural variations on the theme of sex/gender diversity. Androgyny, alternative sexes and genders, gender crossing, transvestism, and gender liminality are defined differently and have different meanings in different societies. In this summary, I compare some of the more important variations.

CRITERIA FOR CONSTRUCTING SEX/GENDER VARIATION

One difference among cultures are the criteria used for constructing diverse sex/gender roles. Genitals are the primary component in some, but not all cultures: genitals are central in Euro-American cultures but anatomy was not a determinant in the traditional Philippines, among Native Americans, or in Polynesia, where cross-gender occupation is more important.

Sexuality is an important criterion in many cultures for sex/gender diversity, though the association is complex and varies across cultures. In the cultures in this text, male sex/gender variants are assumed to take a receptor role in anal sex (or in the case of the māhū, the feminine fellator role), though that connection assumes different significance. In Brazil, Thailand, and the Philippines, the sexual role is sufficiently important so that male gender variants (travestí, kathoey, bakla) may be defined as transgendered homosexuals; the hijra, however, although known *sub rosa* to take this role, are not primarily defined by it. The same is true in American Indian cultures and for Polynesian gender liminals. This evidence argues against any one-way, cause-and-effect relationship between homosexuality and sex/gender diversity, and a specific sexuality may well emerge from a sex/gender variant role, rather than the reverse. On the other hand, sex/gender diversity is widely, if not universally, associated with male same-sex sexual relations, as in contemporary Brazil, Thailand, the Philippines, and eighteenth- and nineteenth-century Europe, and the association cannot be lightly dismissed.

While cross-gender sexuality and accompanying feminine behavior is frequently central in defining male sex/gender variance, for many female gender variants, such as the Indian sādhin, the transvestite saints of the European Middle Ages, and the sworn virgins of the Balkans, it is the renunciation of their sexuality that (re)defines their gender. For American Indian female sex/gender variants, sexuality appears, for the most part, to be irrelevant.

In light of the existing ethnographic record, the soundest conclusion at this time is that the association between sexuality and sex/gender diversity cannot be assumed, but rather must be examined within specific cultural/historical contexts.

Intersexuality (ambiguous genitalia) is important in some cultures as a starting point for gender diversity, but not as frequently as the Euro-American focus on the primacy of genitals in gender would suggest. Hijras, Navajo nádleeh, and the traditional Thai kathoey are the main roles in which biological hermaphroditism is central, though these gender variant roles include other, even more important, behavioral factors.

VARYING DEGREES OF INSTITUTIONALIZATION

Cultures also vary in the extent to which gender diversity is institutionalized, that is, governed by relatively consistent and well-known norms that clearly mark gender variant roles as different from those of man and woman. American Indian cultures most clearly defined their gender variants as having autonomous roles (distinct from that of either man or woman), which were acquired through public rituals.

Hijras occupy a highly institutionalized sex/gender variant role in India. The hijra role involves a formal ritual for initiation, clear behavioral norms that set it apart from other gender roles and that solidify hijras' interactions among themselves. Part of the institutionalization of the hijra role includes local, regional, and even nationwide social networks and communities. Gender variant roles in contemporary Brazil, Polynesia, Thailand, and the Philippines are less institutionalized, but in urban areas, where gender variants congregate to work or live, gender variant subcultures develop, and gender variants are associated with particular roles in those societies.

VARIATION IN PUBLIC RECOGNITION OF
SEX/GENDER TRANSFORMATIONS

Cultures differ in the degree to which they recognize the possibility of complete sex/gender crossing. The Euro-American transsexual exemplifies the most extreme of this recognition: sex-reassignment surgery aims precisely at the reassignment of an individual from one sex to the other. The Mohave hwame and alyha seem closest to the Euro-American transsexual in their desire to be recognized as members of the "opposite" sex. Yet even here, in spite of gender variants' strenuous efforts to imitate the physiological processes of the "other" sex, complete sex/gender transformations were not culturally acknowledged and, indeed to some extent, were ridiculed.

In Brazil, both travestís themselves and the public deny complete sex/gender transformation. Most significantly, travestís do not wish to get rid of their penises, although they go to great lengths to achieve other aspects of female anatomy through the injection of silicone. Travestís control their presentation of their sex/gender role according to their emotional and financial interests. While in deference to the desires of their boyfriends they "background" the penis, they may also use it to satisfy their customers if the price is right. While Brazilians express awe regarding the feminine beauty of successful travestís, they also try to shame other travestís by using masculine forms of address, denying their feminine pretensions.

Like travestís, Filipino bakla do not generally undergo sex-reassignment surgery and acknowledge the impossibility of becoming women because they cannot bear children. Yet, in their feminine presentations of self, particularly in beauty contests, bakla gender transformations aim at perfection. Indeed, many Filipino women agree that bakla, in their appropriation of international images of glamour and style, are more successful than ordinary women. At the same time, however, the underlying audience awareness of the bakla sex/gender transformation as a transformation is always present in bakla spectacles, and the possibility of a "gender slip" generates a certain amount of tension for contestants and for the audience.

In a very different context, the sworn virgin of the Balkans also is not viewed as a complete gender transformation. Social recognition of the gender change is observed out of respect for the individual's wishes and to accord a family the honor of having continued its "house," but there are occasions, such as Tonë's funeral or the prohibition on killing even an armed sworn virgin, when the acceptance of the sex/gender transformation breaks down.

The Euro-American phenomenon of the complete sex crossover of the transsexual was made possible by the improvement of the medical technology of sex-reassignment surgery. A question arises: If the technology were available, would the partial gender crossing in other cultures be transformed into transsexualism? Evidence is not available to answer this question. While the sex-reassignment surgery of Roberta Close, the most celebrated Brazilian travestí, indicates the possibility, as does the apparently increasing desire for sex-reassignment surgery among Filipino bakla, some Euro-American transgenderists and intersexuals reject that technology, preferring to live androgynously.

EXPLAINING SEX/GENDER DIVERSITY

There are several different perspectives for examining the cultural/ historical conditions under which sex/gender diversity emerges. *Gender differentiation* has been suggested as one significant factor. Gender differentiation refers to the extent to which gender roles in a society are well defined, specialized, and hierarchical as opposed to fluid, overlapping, and egalitarian. Two studies that attempted to answer this question were inconclusive: sex/gender diversity was found in cultures with both high and low gender differentiation (Munroe and Munroe 1977; Munroe, Whiting, and Hally 1969). Our ethnographic evidence here is also inconclusive. India is a culture with high gender differentiation, yet it also contains several gender variant roles; in contrast, many American Indian cultures that have (relatively) low gender differentiation also have a high degree of sex/gender diversity. Similarly, gender diversity appears not only in Polynesia and traditional Thailand, where gender differentiation is relatively low (though perhaps not as low as Western observers have reported), but also in Brazil where gender differentiation is very high. Whereas Unni Wikan (1977) attributes the emergence of the male gender variant, xanith, in the Arab sultanate of Oman, to high gender variation, Evelyn Blackwood (1984) attributes a high number of female American Indian gender variants to relatively low gender differentiation in those cultures.

Sex/gender diversity may be associated with a particular cultural concept of the person. In India, for example, the concept of dharma allows for behavioral flexibility according to each individual's unique situation and past experiences, and sex/gender diversity is viewed as one among many legitimate life paths. Regarding the xanith, Omani culture holds that the world is imperfect; people are created with dissimilar natures and are likewise imperfect, and the gender nonconformist is tolerated and allowed to pursue his or her life in peace. In Polynesian and American Indian cultures also, there is less concern with forcing individuals into a mold into which they do not fit, whether by physical anomaly or personal inclination; sex/gender diversity is considered natural and is not subject to moral or legal sanctions. In Polynesia and Thailand, the cultural focus on how individuals play their social roles means that private behavior that does not impinge on social order is largely left alone.

Worldview, or cosmology, seems particularly associated with the presence or absence of sex/gender diversity. In the Philippines, in American Indian cultures, in Afro-Brazilian (and West African) religions, and in Hindu India, the possibility, and even the power, of transformations is a cultural pattern congenial to the emergence of sex/gender diversity. Androgyny—and indeed, other roles or symbols that combine or mediate between two categories—is a powerful symbol in many cultures, often connected with the origin of human beings. Where androgyny is sacred, as in Hinduism and in island Southeast Asia, conditions for the emergence of sex/gender diversity seem favorable.

MALE AND FEMALE GENDER DIVERSITY

I have already noted the preponderance of male, compared to female, sex/gender variant roles. Several different, but not necessarily mutually exclusive, explanations are suggestive. Psychological explanations focus on the more contingent nature of the development of masculinity. Since both males and females are brought up by women, children have a high degree of identification with female gender roles. The development of a mature masculine identity therefore requires a separation from the female, which is not as compelling for the development of feminine identity. Social explanations highlight the fact that in patriarchal societies, women gain social status by acting like men, while men lose social status by acting like women. Female-to-male gender transformations thus make "social sense" and present less of a "crisis" for the social order than male-to-female transformations. And as noted earlier, some of the imbalance may be due to the androcentric (male-centered) nature of the social sciences, particularly psychology.

THE FUNCTIONS, ROLES, AND SIGNIFICANCE OF SEX/GENDER DIVERSITY

As noted throughout this text, sex/gender diversity is associated with special functions in many societies. American Indian gender variants had special functions in their societies that were often associated with their in-between status, such as healing sexual diseases or serving

as go-betweens in marriage. Hijras, too, have special ritual roles at childbirth and marriage; as persons unable to procreate themselves, they paradoxically have the power, through their identification with the Mother
Goddess, to confer fertility on others. The mixed gender of the Brazilian
bicha also associates them with the sacred transformations involved in
trance in Afro-Brazilian religions. While contemporary Polynesian and
Filipino sex/gender variants are not endowed with specifically sacred
powers, they do have secular ritual roles: in Polynesia they are role models of what a man or a virgin girl should not be and represent the spontaneous and the unruly in contrast to the norms of restraint; while in the
Philippines, the bakla mediate between local and international cultural
systems of beauty and style.

The extent to which sex/gender variants represent challenges to
sex/gender binaries is a subject of debate. On the one hand, sex/gender
variants like the Brazilian travestí, the Philippine bakla, or the Euro-
American transsexual or "drag queen" appear to reinforce the heterogender, patriarchal sex/gender ideologies in their respective societies, no
matter how much they may resist negative stereotypes on a personal
level or actively manipulate these stereotypes in adapting to society. On
the other hand, some gender theorists hold that the cross-gender behavior of sex/gender variants, however seemingly humorous, playful, or
marginalized, is always subversive, in that it calls attention to the social
construction of sex and gender (Butler 1990; Garber 1992; Newton 1979).
Yet a third position holds that in some societies, such as the precontact
Philippines, Polynesia, native North America, and in traditional Buddhist or Hindu religious thought, the debate is misguided because sex/
gender diversity and sex/gender transformations are considered to be as
"natural" as the sex/gender roles of male and female. Anthropology
makes its contribution to this debate by joining theory to the observed
richness and variety of the human experience across cultures as this is
documented in the ethnographic record.

Glossary

alyha. Male gender variant among the Mohave Indians.

androgyny. The uniting of male and female.

bayot/bakla/bantut. Transgendered male role in the Philippines.

Candomble. An Afro-Brazilian religion in which women and gender variants play important leadership roles.

dharma. Literally, duty; the Hindu belief that all individuals must follow their own life path to salvation, based on their own personal qualities and social role.

gender. The qualities and roles associated with femininity, masculinity, and alternative roles in a particular society.

gender differentiation. The extent to which gender roles in a society are specialized and hierarchical or fluid and egalitarian.

gender diversity (gender variation). Sex/gender systems that contain more than male and female, masculine and feminine categories.

gendered homosexuality. A sex/gender ideology in which males who take the receptor role in same-sex sexual relations are also expected to, and do, adopt feminine behaviors.

hermaphrodite. A person born with male and female genitalia.

heterosexual. A person whose sexual orientation entails sexual desires toward a person of the opposite sex.

hijra. A male sex/gender variant in India, neither man nor woman.

homosexuality (contemporary Western). A sexual orientation toward a person of the same sex/gender.

hwame. A female gender variant among the Mohave.

intersexuality. A condition in which an individual is born with ambiguous genitalia.

kathoey. A Thai gender variant, originally meaning hermaphrodite but now mainly referring to transgendered males.

māhū. A primarily male gender variant in Tahiti.

molly. The illegitimate male gender variant in eighteenth-century England, practicing sodomy and adopting feminine behaviors.

nádleeh. The designation of a variety of sex/gender variants among the Navajo.

sādhin. A female gender variant associated with virginity in India.

sapphist. An (illegitimate) female gender variant role in eighteenth-century London defined mainly by the adoption of masculine behavior.

sex. The biological aspects of being male, female or other.

sex/gender identity. The relatively consistent, subjective experiencing of oneself as male or female, feminine or masculine, or other.

sexual orientation. A sexual preference for a partner of the same or opposite sex.

sexuality. Can refer to sexual orientation or sexual practices.

sworn virgin. A female-to-male transgendered role in the Balkans.

transgenderists (transpeople). An inclusive sex/gender category in Euro-American societies that includes both transsexuals and others who keep both their feminine and masculine characteristics.

transsexual (in Euro-American culture). A person convinced he/she belongs to the gender opposite to that of his/her anatomy (postoperative: a transsexual who undergoes sex-reassignment surgery).

transvestite. One who cross-dresses (either sporadically or permanently, and for different psychological or cultural reasons).

travestí (bicha, viado). A male transgendered role in Brazil.

two-spirit. A widespread contemporary label for Native American male and female gender variants, previously called berdache.

References

denotes ethnographies particularly appropriate for students for further research

Albers, Patricia C. 1989. "From Illusion to Illumination: Anthropological Studies of American Indian Women." In *Gender and Anthropology: Critical Reviews for Research and Teaching,* edited by Sandra Morgen. Washington, DC: American Anthropological Association.

Amadiume, Ifi. 1987. *Male Daughters, Female Husbands.* Atlantic Highlands, NJ: Zed Books.

Angier, Natalie. 1997. "New Debate over Surgery on Genitals." *New York Times,* May 13, p. C1.

Anson, John. 1974. "The Female Transvestite in Early Monasticism: The Origin and Development of a Motif." *Viator: Medieval and Renaissance Studies* 5, p. 30.

Besnier, Niko. 1996. "Polynesian Gender Liminality through Time and Space." In *Third Sex, Third Gender: Beyond Sexual Dimorphism in Culture and History,* edited by Gilbert Herdt. New York: Zone (MIT), pp. 285–328.

———. 1997. "Sluts and Superwomen: The Politics of Gender Liminality in Urban Tonga." *Ethnos* 62 (1–2): 5–31.

Blackwood, Evelyn. 1984. "Sexuality and Gender in Certain Native American Tribes: The Case of Cross-Gender Females." *Signs: Journal of Women in Culture and Society* 10:1–42.

Blackwood, Evelyn, and Saskia E. Wieringa. 1999. *Female Desires: Same-Sex Relations and Transgender Practices across Cultures.* New York: Columbia University Press.*

Bolin, Anne. 1988. *In Search of Eve: Transsexual Rites of Passage.* South Hadley, MA: Bergin and Garvey.*

———. 1996a. "Transcending and Transgendering: Male-to-Female Transsexuals, Dichotomy and Diversity." In *Third Sex, Third Gender: Beyond Sexual Dimorphism in Culture and History,* edited by Gilbert Herdt, pp. 447–86. New York: Zone (MIT).

———. 1996b. "Traversing Gender: Cultural Context and Gender Practices." In *Gender Reversals and Gender Cultures,* edited by Sabrina Petra Ramet, pp. 22–51. London and New York: Routledge.

Brandes, Stanley. 1981. "Like Wounded Stags: Male Sexual Ideology in an An-
    dalusian Town." In *Sexual Meanings: The Cultural Construction of Gender
    and Sexuality*, edited by Sherry B. Ortner and Harriet Whitehead, pp. 216–
    39. Cambridge: Cambridge University Press.
Buchanan, Scott, ed. 1977. *The Portable Plato*. New York, Penguin.
Bullough, Vern L., and Bonnie Bullough. 1993. *Cross Dressing, Sex, and Gender*.
    Philadelphia: University of Pennsylvania Press.
Butler, Judith. 1990. *Gender Trouble: Feminism and the Subversion of Identity*.
    New York and London: Routledge.
Callender, Charles, and Lee M. Kochems. 1983. "The North American Berdache."
    Current Anthropology 24 (4): 443–56 (Commentary, pp. 456–70).
Cannell, Fenella. 1995. "The Power of Appearances: Beauty, Mimicry and Trans-
    formation in Bicol." In *Discrepant Histories: Translocal Essays on Filipino
    Cultures*, edited by V. Rafael. Manila: Anvil Publishing.
———. 1999. *Power and Intimacy in the Christian Philippines*. Cambridge: Cam-
    bridge University Press.
Chodorow, Nancy. 1974. "Family Structure and Feminine Personality." In *Wom-
    en, Culture, and Society*, edited by M. Rosaldo and L. Lamphere, pp. 43–66.
    Stanford: Stanford University Press.
Cohen, Colleen Ballerino, Richard Wilk, and Beverly Stoeltje, eds. 1996. *Beauty
    Queens on the Global Stage: Gender, Contests, and Power*. New York: Rout-
    ledge.
Cohen, Lawrence. 1995. "The Pleasures of Castration: The Postoperative Status
    of Hijras, Jankhas and Academics." In *Sexual Nature, Sexual Culture*, edited
    by Paul R. Abramson and Steven D. Pinkerton, pp. 276–304. Chicago: Uni-
    versity of Chicago Press.
Connor, Randy P. 1996. *Blossom of Bone*. San Francisco: Harper.
Cornwall, Andrea. 1994. "Gendered Identities and Gender Ambiguity among
    Travestís in Salvador, Brazil." In *Dislocating Masculinity: Comparative Eth-
    nographies*, edited by Andrea Cornwall and Nancy Lindisfarne, pp. 111–32.
    London: Routledge.
Devereux, George. 1937. "Institutionalized Homosexuality of the Mohave Indi-
    ans." *Human Biology* 9:498–587.
Dreger, Alice Domurat. 1998. *Hermaphrodites and the Medical Invention of Sex*.
    Cambridge: Harvard University Press.
Elliston, Deborah A. 1999. "Negotiating Transitional Sexual Economies: Female
    Māhū and Same-Sex Sexuality in 'Tahiti and Her Islands.'" In *Female De-
    sires: Same-Sex Relations and Transgender Practices Across Cultures*, edited
    by Evelyn Blackwood and Saskia E. Wieringa, pp. 230–52. New York: Co-
    lumbia University Press.
Epstein, Julia, and Kristina Straub, eds. 1991. *Body Guards: The Cultural Poli-
    tics of Gender Ambiguity*. New York: Routledge.
Errington, S. 1990. "Recasting Sex, Gender and Power: Theoretical Introduction
    and Regional Overview." In *Power and Difference: Gender in Island South-
    east Asia*. Stanford, CA: Stanford University Press.
Fausto-Sterling, Anne. 1993. "The Five Sexes: Why Male and Female Are Not
    Enough." *The Sciences*, March–April, pp. 20–24.
Feinberg, Leslie. 1996. *Transgender Warriors: Making History from Joan of Arc
    to RuPaul*. Boston: Beacon.*

Fry, Peter. 1986. "Male Homosexuality and Spirit Possession in Brazil." In *Anthropology and Homosexual Behavior*, edited by Evelyn Blackwood, pp. 137–54. New York and London: Haworth Press.

———. 1995. "Male Homosexuality and Afro-Brazilian Possession Cults." In *Latin American Male Homosexualities*, edited by Stephen O. Murray, pp. 193–220. Albuquerque: University of New Mexico.

Fulton, Robert, and Steven W. Anderson. 1992. "The Amerindian 'Man-Woman': Gender, Liminality, and Cultural Continuity." *Current Anthropology* 33 (5): 603–10.

Garber, Majorie. 1992. *Vested Interests: Cross Dressing and Cultural Anxiety*. New York: Routledge, Chapman, and Hall.*

Garcia, Neil C. 1996. *Philippine Gay Culture: The Last 30 Years: Binabae to Bakla, Silahis to MSM*. Quezon City, Philippines: University of the Philippines Press.*

Gilmore, David D. 1990. *Manhood in the Making: Cultural Concepts of Masculinity*. New Haven: Yale University Press.

———. 1996. "Above and Below: Toward a Social Geometry of Gender." *American Anthropologist* 98 (1): 34–66.

Goffman, Erving. 1963. *Stigma: Notes on the Management of Spoiled Identity*. Engelwood Cliffs, NJ: Prentice-Hall.

Gregg, Joan. 1997. *Devils, Women, and Jews: Reflections of the Other in Medieval Sermon Stories*. Albany: State University of New York.

Gremaux, Rene. 1996. "Woman Becomes Man in the Balkans." In *Third Sex, Third Gender: Beyond Sexual Dimorphism in Culture and History*, edited by Gilbert Herdt, pp. 241–84. New York: Zone (MIT).

Hall, Kira. 1995. "Hijra/Hijrin: Language and Gender Identity." Unpublished doctoral dissertation in Linguistics, University of California, Berkeley. Ann Arbor, MI: UMI Dissertation Services.

———. 1997. "'Go Suck Your Husband's Sugarcane!': Hijras and the Use of Sexual Insult." In *Queerly Phrased: Language, Gender, and Sexuality*, edited by Anna Livia and Kira Hall, pp. 430–60. New York: Oxford.

Hayes, Kelley. 1996. *Meu Querido Viado: Gender and Possession Trance in Candomble*. Unpublished ms.

Hekma, Gert. 1996. "'A Female Soul in a Male Body': Sexual Inversion as Gender Inversion in Nineteenth-Century Sexology." In *Third Sex, Third Gender: Beyond Sexual Dimorphism in Culture and History*, edited by Gilbert Herdt, pp. 212–40. New York: Zone (MIT).

Herdt, Gilbert. 1981. *Guardians of the Flutes: Idioms of Masculinity*. New York: McGraw Hill.

———. 1996a. "Introduction: Third Sexes and Third Genders." In *Third Sex, Third Gender: Beyond Sexual Dimorphism in Culture and History*, edited by Gilbert Herdt, pp. 21–81. New York: Zone (MIT).

———. 1996b. "Mistaken Sex: Culture, Biology and the Third Sex in New Guinea." In *Third Sex, Third Gender: Beyond Sexual Dimorphism in Culture and History*, edited by Gilbert Herdt, pp. 419–46. New York: Zone (MIT).

Hill, Willard W. 1935. "The Status of the Hermaphrodite and Transvestite in Navaho Culture." *American Anthropologist* 37:273–79.

Hiltelbeitel, Alf. 1980. "Siva, the Goddess, and the Disguises of the Pandavas and Draupadi." *History of Religions* 20 (1–2): 147–74.

Humes, Cynthia Ann. 1996. "Becoming Male: Salvation through Gender Modification in Hinduism and Buddhism." In *Gender Reversals and Gender Cultures: Anthropological and Historical Perspectives*, edited by Sabrina Petra Ramet, pp. 123–37. London: Routledge,

Jacobs, Sue-Ellen, Wesley Thomas, and Sabine Lang, eds. 1997. *Two-Spirit People: Native American Gender Identity, Sexuality, and Spirituality*. Urbana and Chicago: University of Illinois.

Jackson, Peter. 1997a. "*Kathoey*><Gay> <Man: The Historical Emergence of Gay Male Identity in Thailand." In *Sites of Desire: Economies of Pleasure: Sexualities in Asia and the Pacific*, edited by Lenore Manderson and Margaret Jolly, pp. 166–90. Chicago: University of Chicago.

———. 1997b. "Thai Research on Male Homosexuality and Transgenderism and the Cultural Limits of Foucaultian Analysis." *Journal of the History of Sexuality* 8 (1): 52–85.

———. 1995. *Dear Uncle Go: Male Homosexuality in Thailand*. Bangkok: Bua.

Johnson, Mark. 1996. "Negotiating Style and Mediating Beauty: Transvestite (*Gay/Bantut*) Beauty Contests in the Southern Philippines." In *Beauty Queens on the Global Stage: Gender, Contests, and Power*, edited by Colleen Ballerino Cohen, Richard Wilk, and Beverly Stoeltje, pp. 89–104. New York: Routledge.

———. 1997. *Beauty and Power: Transgendering and Cultural Transformation in the Southern Philippines*. New York: Berg.*

Kakar, Sudhir. 1982. *Shamans, Mystics and Doctors: A Psychological Inquiry into India and Its Healing Traditions*. New York: Knopf.

Kessler, Suzanne J. 1998. *Lessons from the Intersexed*. Piscataway, NJ: Rutgers University Press.

Kessler, Suzanne J. and Wendy McKenna. 1978. *Gender: An Ethnomethodological Approach*. New York: Wiley.

Kogan, Terry S. 1997. "Transsexuals and Critical Gender Theory: The Possibility of a Restroom Labeled 'Other.'" *Hastings Law Journal* 48 (6): 1223–55.

Kottack, Conrad. 1990. "Hidden Women, Public Men—Public Women, Hidden Men." In *Gender Transformations*, edited by Janise Hurtig and Kate Gillogly, pp. 57–60. *Michigan Discussions in Anthropology* 9, Spring. Ann Arbor, MI.

Kulick, Don. 1996. "Causing a Commotion: Scandal as Resistance among Brazilian Travestí Prostitutes." *Anthropology Today* 12 (6): 3–7.

———. 1997. "The Gender of Brazilian Transgendered Prostitutes." *American Anthropologist* 99 (3): 574–85.

———. 1998. *Travestí: Sex, Gender and Culture among Brazilian Transgendered Prostitutes*. Chicago: University of Chicago Press.

Landes, Ruth. 1946. *The City of Women*. New York: Macmillan.

Lang, Sabine. 1996. "There Is More than Just Men and Women: Gender Variance in North America." In *Gender Reversals and Gender Culture*, edited by Sabrina Petra Ramet, pp. 183–96. London and New York: Routledge

———. 1998. *Men as Women, Women as Men: Changing Gender in Native American Cultures*. Trans. from the German by John L. Vantine. Austin: University of Texas Press.

Lannoy, Richard. 1975. *The Speaking Tree*. New York: Oxford University Press.

Laqueur, Thomas. 1990. *Making Sex: Body and Gender from the Greeks to Freud.* Cambridge, MA: Harvard University Press.

Levy, Robert. 1973. *Tahitians: Mind and Experience in the Society Islands.* Chicago: University of Chicago.

Lothstein, Leslie Martin. 1983. *Female-to-Male Transsexualism: Historical, Clinical and Theoretical Issues.* Boston: Routledge and Kegan Paul.

Mageo, Jeannette Marie. 1992. "Male Transvestism and Cultural Change in Samoa." *American Ethnologist* 9 (3): 443–59.

Magerl, Gabriela. 2000. *Waria: A Third Gender in Indonesia.* Unpublished manuscript. University of Vienna, Austria.

Manalansan, Martin F. IV. 1995. "Speaking of AIDS: Language and the Filipino 'Gay' Experience in America." In *Discrepant Histories: Translocal Essays on Filipino Cultures*, edited by Vicente L. Rafael. Philadelphia: Temple University Press.

———. 1997. "In the Shadows of Stonewall: Examining Gay Transnational Politics and the Diasporic Dilemma." In *The Politics of Culture in the Shadow of Capital*, edited by Lisa Lowe and David Lloyd, pp. 485–585. Durham, NC: Duke University Press.

Matory, J. Lorand. 1994. *Sex and the Empire That Is No More: Gender and the Politics of Metaphor in Oyo Yoruba Religion.* Minneapolis: University of Minnesota Press.

———. 1996. *Man in the City of Women.* Unpublished ms.

Mead, Margaret. 1971. *Coming of Age in Samoa.* New York: Morrow.

Medicine, Beatrice. 1983. "Warrior Women: Sex Role Alternatives for Plains Indian Women." In *The Hidden Half: Studies of Plains Indian Women*, edited by P. Albers and B. Medicine, pp. 267–80. Lanham Park, MD: University Press of America.

Money, John, and Anke A. Ehrhardt. 1972. *Man and Woman, Boy and Girl.* Baltimore, MD: Johns Hopkins Press.

Morris, R. C. 1994. "Three Sexes and Four Sexualities: Redressing the Discourses on Sexuality and Gender in Thailand." *Positions* 2 (1): 15–43.

Munroe, Robert L., and Ruth H. Munroe. 1977. "Male Transvestism and Subsistence Economy." *Journal of Social Psychology* 103:307–8.

Munroe, Robert L., John W. M. Whiting, and David J. Hally. 1969. "Institutionalized Male Transvestism and Sex Distinction." *American Anthropologist* 71:87–91.

Murray, Stephen O. 1995. *Latin American Male Homosexualities.* Albuquerque: University of New Mexico Press.

Murray, Stephen O., and Will Roscoe. 1997. *Islamic Homosexualities: Culture, History, and Literature.* New York: New York University Press.

Nanda, Serena. 1996. "Hijras: An Alternative Sex and Gender Role in India." In *Third Sex, Third Gender: Beyond Sexual Dimorphism in Culture and History*, edited by Gilbert Herdt, pp. 373–418. New York: Zone (MIT).

———. 1999. *The Hijras of India: Neither Man nor Woman*, 2nd. ed. Belmont, CA.: Wadsworth.*

Newton, Esther. 1979. *Mother Camp: Female Impersonators in America.* Chicago: University of Chicago Press.*

Oboler, Regina Smith. 1980. "Is the Female Husband a Man? Woman/Woman Marriage among the Nandi of Kenya." *Ethnology* 19 (1): 69–88.

O'Flaherty, Wendy Doniger. 1973. *Siva: The Erotic Ascetic*. New York: Oxford.
——. 1980. *Women, Androgynes, and Other Mythical Beasts*. Chicago: University of Chicago Press.
Ostor, Akos, Lina Fruzetti, and Steve Barnett, eds. 1982. *Concepts of Person: Kinship, Caste, and Marriage in India*. Cambridge, MA: Harvard University Press.
Parker, Richard C. 1991. *Bodies, Pleasure, and Passions: Sexual Culture in Contemporary Brazil*. Boston: Beacon Press.
——. 1995. Changing Brazilian Constructions of Homosexuality. In *Latin American Male Homosexualities*, edited by Stephen O. Murray, pp. 241–55. Albuquerque: University of New Mexico Press,
——. 1999. " 'Within Four Walls': Brazilian Sexual Culture and HIV/AIDS." In *Culture, Society and Sexuality*, edited by Richard Parker and Peter Aggleton, pp. 253–66. London: UCL Press.
Peacock, James. 1968. *Rites of Modernization: Symbolic Aspects of Indonesian Proletarian Drama*. Chicago: University of Chicago Press.
Penrose, Walter. 2001. "Hidden in History: Female Homoeroticism and Women of a 'Third Nature' in the South Asian Past." *Journal of the History of Sexuality* 10 (1): 3–39.
Phillimore, Peter. 1991. "Unmarried Women of the Dhaula Dhar: Celibacy and Social Control in Northwest India." *Journal of Anthropological Research* 47 (3): 331–50.
Preston, Laurence W. 1987. "A Right to Exist: Eunuchs and the State in Nineteenth-Century India." *Modern Asian Studies* 21 (2): 371–87.
Ranade, S. N. 1983. *A Study of Eunuchs in Delhi*. Unpublished manuscript. Government of India, Delhi.
Roller, Lynn E. 1999. *In Search of God the Mother: The Cult of Aatolian Cybele*. Berkeley: University of California Press.
Roscoe, Will. 1991. *The Zuni Man-Woman*. Albuquerque: University of New Mexico Press.*
——. 1995. "Cultural Anesthesia and Lesbian and Gay Studies." *American Anthropologist* 97 (3): 448–52.
——. 1996. "How to Become a Berdache: Toward a Unified Analysis of Gender Diversity." In *Third Sex, Third Gender: Beyond Sexual Dimorphism in Culture and History*, edited by Gilbert Herdt, pp. 329–72. New York: Zone (MIT).
——. 1998. *Changing Ones: Third and Fourth Genders in Native North America*. London: Macmillan.
Roscoe, Will, and Stephen O. Murray, eds. 1998. *Boy-Wives and Female-Husbands: Studies in African Homosexualities*. New York: St. Martins.
Shapiro, Judith. 1991. "Transsexualism: Gender and the Mutability of Sex." In *Body Guards: The Cultural Politics of Gender Ambiguity*, edited by Julia Epstein and Kristina Straub, pp. 248–78. New York: Routledge.
Schaeffer, Claude E. 1965. "The Kutenai Female Berdache: Courier Guide, and Warrior." *Ethnohistory: The Bulletin of the Ohio Valley Historic Indian Conference* 12 (3): 173–236.
Shore, Bradd. 1981. "Sexuality and Gender in Samoa: Conceptions and Missed Conceptions." In *Sexual Meanings: The Cultural Construction of Gender and Sexuality*, edited by Sherry B. Ortner and Harriet Whitehead, pp. 192–215. Cambridge: Cambridge University Press.
Singh, Kushwant. 1990. *Delhi: A Novel*. New Delhi: Penguin.

Sullivan, Gerard, and Laurence Wai-Teng Leong, eds. 1995. *Gays and Lesbians in Asia and the Pacific: Social and Human Services*. New York: The Haworth Press.

Thomas, Wesley. 1997. "Navajo Cultural Constructions of Gender and Sexuality." In *Two-Spirit People: Native American Gender Identity, Sexuality, and Spirituality*, edited by Sue-Ellen Jacobs, Wesley Thomas, and Sabine Lang, pp. 156–73. Urbana and Chicago: University of Illinois.

Trumbach, Randolph. 1996. "London's Sapphists: From Three Sexes to Four Genders in the Making of Modern Culture." In *Third Sex, Third Gender: Beyond Sexual Dimorphism in Culture and History*, edited by Gilbert Herdt, pp. 111–36. New York: Zone (MIT).

———. 1998. *Sex and the Gender Revolution*. Vol. 1 of *Heterosexuality and the Third Gender in Enlightenment London*. Chicago: University of Chicago Press.

Turner, Victor. 1969. *The Ritual Process: Structure and Anti-structure*. Ithaca: Cornell University.

Wafer, James. 1991. *The Taste of Blood: Spirit Possession in Brazilian Candomble*. Philadelphia: University of Pennsylvania Press.

Whitam, Frederick L. 1992. "Bayot and Callboy: Homosexual-Heterosexual Relations in the Philippines." In *Oceanic Homosexualities*, edited by Stephen O. Murray, pp. 231–48. New York: Garland.

Whitehead, Harriet. 1981. "The Bow and the Burden Strap: A New Look at Institutionalized Homosexuality in Native North America." In *Sexual Meanings: the Cultural Construction of Gender and Sexuality*, edited by Sherry B. Ortner and Harriet Whitehead, pp. 80–115. Cambridge: Cambridge University Press.

Wikan, Unni. 1977. "Man Becomes Woman: Transsexualism in Oman as a Key to Gender Roles." *Man*, N.S. 12:304–19.

Williams, Walter. 1992. *The Spirit and the Flesh: Sexual Diversity in American Indian Culture*. Boston: Beacon.

Zwilling, L., and M. Sweet. 1996. "Like a City Ablaze: The Third Sex and the Creation of Sexuality in Jain Religious Literature." *Journal of the History of Sexuality* 6 (3): 359–84.

———. 2000. "The Evolution of Third Sex Constructs in Ancient India: A Study in Ambiguity." In *Constructing Ideologies: Religion, Gender, and Social Definition in India*, edited by Julia Leslie, pp. 99–133. Delhi: Oxford University Press.

Selected Films

The Adventures of Priscilla, Queen of the Desert. Director, Stephan Elliott. 1994. Gramercy Pictures. Color. 102 minutes. A wonderfully moving and funny film about three "drag queens" on an odyssey across the Australian desert. Movies Unlimited, 3015 Darnell Road, Philadelphia, PA 19154.

Bombay Eunuch. Alexandra Shiva. 2001. Color. Digital video. 71 minutes. In Hindi and Tamil with English subtitles. An interesting, very contemporary documentary film on a group of hijras in Bombay, which illuminates many aspects—sexual, social, and economic—of their lives. Gidalya Pictures, 49 Bleecker Street, Fourth Floor, New York, NY 10012. 212/358-9620.

Eunuchs—India's Third Gender. Michael Yorke. 1991. Under the Sun Series. BBC, London. Color. This highly regarded film focuses on contrasting lifestyles and attitudes of three hijras. It treats the subject generally without sensationalism and reflects the filmmakers' long acquaintance with their subject. For distribution contact BBC-Under the Sun, Clarendon Road, Borehamwood, Hertfordshire WD6 1JF, England. Tel.: 011-4481-207-8202; Fax: 011-4481-207-8980.

Juggling Gender. Tami Gold. 1992. Color. 30 minutes. Performance artist and bearded woman Jennifer Miller begins this documentary about gender stereotypes in the United States. Distributor: Women Make Movies. 212/925-0606.

Ladyboys. Jeremy Marre. 1992. Harcourt Films, London. Color. Video. 51 minutes. A good accompaniment for the chapter on Thailand. The film follows the lives of two young men from a rural area as they join the world of the kathoeys and a career in the transvestite cabarets in tourist

117

centers of Thailand. For distribution contact Ros Ali, TVF International, 375 City Road. London, EC1V 1NA, England. Tel.: 011-4471-837-3000. Fax: 011-4471-833-2185.

Ma Vie en Rose (My Life in Pink). Alain Berliner. 1997. Color. 1 hour, 28 minutes. A charming film about a Belgian middle-class family whose seven-year-old son decides that he would like to be a girl.

Paris Is Burning. Jennie Livingston. 1990. Color. 78 minutes. A critically acclaimed film whose subject is the "voguing" subculture of African-American and Latino gays in New York City. The film also serves as a poignant commentary on American cultural values. Movies Unlimited, 3015 Darnell Road, Philadelphia, PA 19154.

The Salt Mines. Susana Aikin and Carlos Aparicio. 1990. Color. 45 minutes. Spanish with subtitles. Through engaging interviews, a picture emerges of the lives of a group of homeless Latino transvestite prostitutes (similar to the travestí of Brazil) who live in the out-of-service sanitation trucks in New York City, which hold the salt for snow removal in the city.

Shinjuku Boys. Kim Longinotto and Jano Williams. 1995. Color. 16mm. 53 minutes. A compelling documentary film relating the stories of "onnabes," women who live as men and have girlfriends (though they don't usually identify as lesbians) and who work in Shinjuku, Tokyo's pleasure district.

Two-Spirit People: The Berdache Tradition in Native American Culture. Lory Levy, Michel Beauchemin, and Gretchen Vogel. 1991. Gender on a Stick Productions. Color. 23 minutes. An informative and positive view of Native American two-spirit roles, using interviews, historical photographs, and dramatic reenactments.

You Don't Know Dick. Candace Schmerhorn and Bestor Cram. An intelligent assembly of interviews with six "transpeople"—female-to-male transsexuals—each of whom tells a fascinating story about the challenges in constructing a new identity. University of California Extension, Center for Media and Independent Learning, 2000 Center Street, 4th floor, Berkeley, CA 94704.

Index

mations, 18–19
Biomedical concept of homosexuality, 71, 73–74. *See also* Medical
model
Bisexuality, among American Indians, 17
Blackwood, Evelyn, 104
Bligh, Captain, 62–63
Bolin, Anne, 95, 100
Bombay, hijra prostitutes in, 37
Brazil, 5
　Afro-Brazil religions in, 50–55
　attitudes toward gender diver-
　　sity in, 49–50
　candomble and gender diversity
　　in, 52–54
　changing sex/gender ideologies
　　in, 55–56
　colonial plantation slave econ-
　　omy in, 43
　gender ideology in, 44
　language and sex/gender system
　　in, 45
　men and not-men in, 48–49
　sexuality and gender in, 43–56
　travestís, bichas, and viados in,
　　43, 45–48
Britain, hijras under rule in India,
39
Buddhism
　kathoey and, 73
　Theravada, 72

Callboys, in Philippines, 81
Candomble (Macumba) religions,
51–52
　and Brazilian gender diversity,
　　52–54
　pasivos and, 53–54
Castes, hijras and, 36, 37, 39
Catholic Church
　Brazilian social hierarchy and,
　　43
　Philippines and, 79
Chela, among hijras, 38
Cheyenne Indians, hetaneman
　female warriors among, 24
Childbearing, hijras and, 30–31
Christianity

in Philippines, 85
in Polynesia, 69
women in, 44
Cliterodectomy, 99
Clitoris
　cliterodectomy and, 99
　surgical reduction of size, 99–
　　100
Close, Roberta, 49, 50
Clothing
　American Indian transvestism
　　and, 15
　of hijras, 30
　Polynesian gender distinctions
　　of, 63
Cosmology, transformation, ambigu-
　ity, and, 20
Creation myth, hijras and, 31
Criminalization, of hijra emascula-
　tion, 39
Crosscultural perspective, on gen-
　der, 1–2
Cross dressing, by transvestite
　female saints, 90–92
Cross-gender sexuality, 102
Cross-gender sexual relations, 74
Crow Indians, Finds Them and Kills
　Them of, 16, 17
Cult of masculinity, in Melanesia, 57
Culture
　gender roles and, 3
　of Philippines, 79
　sex/gender diversity and, 104–5
Culture contact, sex/gender identity
　and, 6–7

Dancing, in Polynesia, 68–69
Darwinian evolution, 89, 90
Devereux, George, 21
"Deviance," 6
Dharma, 34
"Drag queen," 106
Dress. *See* Clothing

Economic roles, of Polynesian men
　and women, 63
Effeminacy
　of gender liminals, 65
　homosexuality and, 90